"EVEN A FLOWER..."

Learnings on
Emotional Integrity
and Spiritual Breadwinning

Adam Perach

"Even A Flower..."
*Learnings on Emotional Integrity
and Spiritual Breadwinning*

All Rights Reserved © 2000, 2004 by Adam Perach, *LLC*

Perach Press, an imprint of
Adam Perach, Publishers

For information,
address the publisher at:

1117 W. Palm Lane
Phoenix, AZ 85007
or
evenaflower@aol.com

ISBN: 0-9722498-1-8

Printed in the United States of America

To every heart so foolish
as to have no doubt, and
to every mind so arrogant
as to have no faith.

Contents

PART THREE: WORKING WITHOUT A NET

PART FOUR: INTEGRATION

PART ONE

SENSATION

Midrash (Allegory) For Part One:
Adam and Eve's Daring Gambit

When God first envisioned a physical world, *sensation* was what came to Mind. Seeing, hearing, feeling, smelling and tasting. A network of neuroreceptors, hardwired to know light from dark, hot from cold, not-enough from too-much. The idea of consciousness ensconced in matter was a big bang indeed.

What God did not foresee was physicality's potential as a medium for *relation*. It was Adam (on the ground) who conceived of an interpersonal operating system for the sensory mainframe. He asked for and was granted a companion. And there were *two* human prototypes, enjoying the fruits of the Garden.

It takes one for sensation; two for relation. But there was evening and there was morning . . . and Eve seemed redundant. Adam's sight and touch confirmed that like everything else the Lord had made, she too "was good." But her physical attributes did little to assuage his relational malaise.

"There's no such *thing* as loneliness," the serpent chided Adam. "It's all in your oversized, *Homo sapiens* head!" Indeed, in all creation, only Eve shared the quintessentially human instinct, even in physical paradise, to gird sensation with relation. "I feel it too," she whispered. "Something's missing."

Eve knew this without needing to eat from the Tree of Knowledge. She was clear from the outset she'd not embodied for sensation. She wanted to *interact*. To express, in and through the physical, her *extra*-sensory (Image-of-God) Essence.

But relation couldn't manifest, like the human genome, on a mere word from the Creator. Adam and Eve would have to work at this. To make their incipient *feelings* flesh. And keep on breathing life into them.

As if that weren't challenge enough for two newborns, their communicative agenda was beset, from the beginning, with a paradox: Eden's very abundance made it functionally obsolescent the moment relation was thought of. For the essence of relation is the will to share. But in the Garden, Adam and Eve already *had* everything. And only God (not each other) to thank.

That's why Adam had to give up paradise and get a job. He wanted to "bring home the bacon." So he could *share* it . . . with his beloved.

1

The Boy in the Ark

In the beginning, the terms of my relationship with God were clear. My job was to behave; His, to make sure only good things happened to my family and me. The arrangement was so simple (and personal), I even gave Him a nickname—an acronym of all our first initials.

Our synagogue, B'nai Israel, was a grand and mysterious place that went well with my childish theology. Just inside the Negley Avenue entrance, a tunnel-like corridor wound steeply around the sanctuary's perimeter. Its curved slope connoted an ascending pilgrimage, especially for those with little or tired old legs.

At the summit, one came into a cavernous hall, with a high, domed ceiling. Chandeliers in the shape of giant Stars of David twinkled brightly. Down a long center aisle, the rich mahogany Ark rose up 25 feet from the dais, resplendent with gold-painted lions. And hidden behind its sliding wooden doors, then a sheer white curtain, were the sacred Torah scrolls, each ornately garbed and crowned.*

*Each scroll contains the first five books of the Bible, handwritten on parchment.

Once, around age nine, I sneaked into the darkened sanctuary. It was a spooky scene, the only light being the red *Ner Tamid* (Eternal Light) that hung above the Ark. Standing in that awesome space, I wondered what would happen were I to steal a bit farther . . . right up into the Ark itself! Might I then feel like one of God's own Torah scrolls, holy and beloved?

On Saturday mornings, the choir sang from a loft, so high up it evoked an angelic presence. They accompanied the Cantor,* who pled our case with high notes so vigorous they turned his whole face red. Yet when the liturgical mood shifted, he could also beseech God in a sacred falsetto whisper.

We rose to our feet when the Ark was finally opened. As the Cantor reached in to remove one of the Torahs, its silver crown and breastplate jangled in anticipation of the excursion down into the hubbub of the congregation. *"Ki mitziyon teytzey Torah,"* sang the choir—"Out of Zion shall go forth the Law." The Cantor then led a procession around the sanctuary, pausing for those who wished to kiss the Torah . . . and singing majestically all the while.

His voice was my Pied Piper. When I was old enough to take my place in the celestial choir loft, the first thing I had to learn was how to funnel so large an exuberance into just the small sound I was trying to emit. Sometimes, it was all I could do to mouth the words.

*In traditional congregations, the cantor leads the worship service, chanting the prayers in Hebrew.

Singing was thus my first love, but also the source of my earliest disillusionment. For all too soon, it was clear that my vocal reach exceeded my grasp. The solos were going to other members of the youth choir. Then, as my Bar Mitzvah approached, my voice began cracking, unpredictably.

God smiled on me that day, and I made it through in rare form. It was as though I'd been granted a boon—one opportunity to sing decently and uninhibitedly before the ax fell. Thereafter, my adolescent "gap" continued to widen, to the point I simply couldn't produce anything remotely resembling a well-placed tone.

In our high school choir, I distinguished myself not as singer, but as student conductor. I went so far as to take an aptitude test at a local conservatory. The scoring sheet confirmed my facility for pitch, rhythm and such. But the fine print cautioned that first and foremost, an aspiring musician must show distinct vocal or instrumental promise. Someone had placed three asterisks beside the admonition, as if I might have missed it.

At age 17, I went off to Israel. Something I'd said or written had called me to the attention of the Dean of the College of Jewish Studies, on whose recommendation I received a scholarship for a year's study in Jerusalem. On my return, now fluent in Hebrew, I enrolled in a cantorial workshop offered by the Hebrew Union College.

The class met for three hours each Tuesday night, at the synagogue of the cantor-instructor. How strange to see the elaborate prayer modes written out note for note, with English transliteration. I had little trouble mastering the material from a musical or linguistic standpoint. But the karma encrypted on my vocal cords proved immune to perseverance.

Resignedly, I enrolled at Purdue, with a major in political science. I nevertheless inflicted myself on the school's *a cappella* choir and even experimented with a voice class. After a willful semester of vocal calisthenics, I got a "C" in the course—not the tenor high C to which I so aspired. When I protested that I'd done everything the instructor had asked of me, his response was, "Yes I know; but *you* didn't improve."

I did land a part-time cantorial job with a fledgling congregation that helped me pay my way through law school. After which I gave up singing to pursue my second choice for a career.

Law school proved an exhilarating experience, especially in comparison to my undergraduate (liberal arts) studies. Here at last was a subject that truly mattered. The fate of the disputants turned on how we reconciled opposing principles and conflicting social agendas.

I found this a most satisfying integration of abstract reasoning and day-to-day practicality. Unlike my classmates, who largely suffered the curriculum as the price of admission to the bar, I enjoyed the law. For me, it was the transition to earning my living as an attorney that would pose the real challenge.

This was complicated by the fact that halfway through law school, I began exploring spiritual life in formats rather alien to my Jewish upbringing. A lawyer for whom I'd done some summer clerking had invited me along to his regular, Sunday morning yoga lesson. (The teacher turned out to be a religiously observant Jewish woman, who happened to have her own hatha yoga studio.)

On the surface, hatha yoga is a physical discipline, a series of postures and breathing exercises, performed with a high degree of concentration. But more than my spine was flexing and relaxing. With each long, measured breath, my cluttered psyche was unlimbering. By the end of the session, I was in a wonderful, buoyant state—calm, but piquantly alert. So I signed up for my own weekly yoga lessons.

My third year of law school afforded a welcome respite from the stress and competitiveness of the first two years. On the strength of my summer clerking, I'd been offered a permanent position with a prominent firm, a full year ahead of graduation. Thus spared the rigors of job seeking with which my classmates were contending, I fretted less about maintaining my high class standing.

It was during this happy time that I picked up *Autobiography of a Yogi,* by Parmahansa Yogananda. In the life story of this inspired swami, I found an exotic yet vaguely familiar approach to God and religion. Had I not known such reverence myself, years before? Yogananda's writing reminded me of the boy who had wanted to be a Torah scroll. And made me wonder where that child had gone . . . why he'd not progressed to a more mature but no less vital spiritual awareness.

Adolescence, it seems, had disrupted more than my vocal registers. There was now also a disconnect between my intellect and the ceremony that had once so moved me.

Judaism, to be sure, was no less rich in religious symbolism or ethical substance. But my own inner shine—what our sacred objects merely reflect back to us—seemed to have tarnished. A phrase from the Sabbath prayer book comes to mind: *"Chadeysh yameynu kekedem*—Renew our days as of old."

My alienation may indeed have reflected a more widespread Jewish malaise. In the fifties and sixties, we were still reeling from the Holocaust. It's not surprising, at such point in our long history, that personal communion with God (which seemed not to have availed the six million) should have taken a back seat to a more sectarian, less spiritual religious life. The champions of our physical survival were the Zionists. But for most American Jews, whose security militated against emigration to Israel, preservation of the religious culture (what we now call "Jewish continuity") came to be viewed as an end in itself.

But Jewish peoplehood couldn't assuage an emerging generation's more elemental need for faith in God. At this equally critical stage of our personal development, our religious mentors seemed not really to want the job. So when, in typical adolescent fashion, we challenged their theology, they pulled the rug right out from under us: "Fine. How very bright of you to be skeptical. We now ordain *you* the leaders of the religious community!"

In this way, my generation was like the four sons we read of in the Passover *Haggadah:** At first, too young to question; then just capable of rote learning. For a time, we

---

*The manual that sets out the ritual for the Passover meal.

asked (sincerely) what all the ceremony was about. But as our social and intellectual development seemed only to distance us from the purported Object of our ritual practices, our disillusionment fell on deaf ears. Almost inevitably, we became the rebellious child, who asks, provocatively, "What are *you* getting out of all this religious mumbo jumbo?"

If the Orthodox measure of Jewish living was the dutiful performance of *mitzvot* (religious commandments), for the less observant majority, it was Jewish charitable work or communal activity (usually centered around support for the State of Israel). Jewish leadership fell to those who could articulate the "Jewish point of view" on a given subject— with poise, verbal clarity and mental conviction. Like good lawyers, in short. But neither the curriculum nor the modeling informed of a direct, personal or life-influencing relationship with God.

I know even as I write such a phrase that it will make many Jews cringe, connoting something alien to our mainstream Jewish culture. This, I think, makes my very point. In spite of our post-Emancipation discomfort with such a notion, pious Jews from Abraham forward have had, at the center of their identities, just such a relationship with (or at least a yearning for) *"Hashem."**

Now here in my third year of law school, I had all the qualifications to take my place as an active, indeed prominent member of the adult Jewish community. I had the birthright and the education. I could articulate Rabbi Kap-

---

*Hebrew for the unspeakable name of God.

lan's* theory of God as "the Power that makes for salvation"—even if I couldn't apply it in any personally useful way. What I hadn't learned from my Judaic curriculum was how to experience a sense of relationship with my Creator.

But some ancient signal, apperceived by the young boy standing in awe before the Holy Ark, now flickered again, like a personal *Ner Tamid*. And for the moment, Swami Yogananda was its unlikely custodian.

*Mordechai Kaplan, founder of the Reconstructionist branch of Judaism.

2

Signs and Wonders

Yogananda stressed that it was possible to know God experientially, not just metaphorically. I'd seen this in tracts handed out by missionaries of various stripe (which I'd dismissed as so much self-delusion on their part). Perhaps what was different about Yogananda's message was that he was telling the story of his own life, not threatening me with eternal damnation. In all events, my circumstances now allowed me the time and energy for some spiritual experimentation.

One day, after an hour or so of yoga postures and deep breathing, I felt particularly alert and focused. "Why not give it a try?" I asked myself. "Give what a try?" I answered. "You know, the talking to *God* thing."

Since no one was looking, I allowed myself, just barely, to continue along these lines. I did some more deep breathing and found my attention gathered at the spot between the eyebrows, sometimes called the "third eye." I fancied myself putting out a signal-beam to God's 1-800 number: "Okay, I'm here. I'm skeptical. (In fact, if ever asked, I'll probably deny we *had* this conversation.) But if You're there and willing to make contact, I'd welcome some unambiguous response."

Yogananda, I remembered, had a guru to help him make the divine connection. Indeed, he'd seen the face of his spiritual teacher in meditation before meeting him in the flesh. Willing to settle for such a sign, I began conjuring up visages of current-day holy people whose names I'd seen on placards or in books.

"What if asking for this kind of thing (or even 'being open to it') means I've already *half lost my mind?"* I panicked. "Oh give it a rest," some more adventuresome part of me prodded. "You'll either get some kind of response or you won't."

Pressing ahead, I tried to visualize someone walking toward me—an item of clothing or some unique ornament by which I might later recognize my spiritual teacher. The image came to mind of a large, red flower.

After half an hour or so, it occurred to me that this was the first real praying I had done since my childhood, in the sense of directing a message to God while entertaining the possibility He might actually hear and respond. I was skeptical, but I was doing it. Not as a ritual and not for public consumption. As some Christians might have put it, I was "knocking."

It also seemed clear that the images passing through my mind during this prayer-meditation were products of my own invention. In fact, I got up from the exercise rather disappointed that nothing whatever had been accomplished.

That evening, I stopped by a relative's house, where a distant cousin was visiting from England. I had no other information about him and no particular expectations for the encounter. But I soon learned it was no mere holiday that had brought Cousin Jeff to America. He'd come all this way to attend a "festival," at the Houston Astrodome . . . with a fourteen year old *guru* named Deva Ji!

I'd seen this kid's picture on posters near the Purdue campus. In fact, he was one of the guru-candidates I'd thought of during my meditation! Six hours later, my hitherto unknown cousin was commending him to me, in terms Yogananda himself might have used: the current *Satguru* (true teacher)—whose very job was to open my inner eye . . . so that I might *know God for myself.*

"I'm not proposing you *believe* in Gurudeva Ji," Jeff pitched me almost irresistibly. "Just give him a chance to show you what he can do. *He'll either deliver or he won't.*"

With the benefit of a quarter-century's hindsight, I can picture God (or some administrative assistant) fielding my call: "What are we going to do for *this* poor guy?" Perhaps they looked quickly around the neighborhood, spotting Gurudeva Ji, in Houston, and Cousin Jeff, with his layover in Chicago. "This is the best we can come up with on short notice; let's just see what he does with it."

Though more than a little intrigued, I never mentioned my meditation earlier in the day nor gave Jeff any inkling what a hot prospect he'd stumbled upon. As I was leaving, he handed me a magazine about the guru to take home. I tossed it onto my coffee table, and it was a day or two before I gave the encounter with my cousin much further thought.

I'm sure I wasn't meditating or otherwise spiritually exerting myself as I sat there on my couch that day. But something drew my attention, almost magnetically, to the picture on the magazine's cover. I felt my head rotate slightly to the left, as though of its own accord. Just enough for my gaze to fall upon the gaudy *red flower* leaping out at me from the guru's lapel!

Now in twenty some years of attending religious services and reciting rote prayers, I'd never had such an experience. Word of other people's cosmic encounters with Gurudeva Ji added fuel to my fire, and in short order, I too was singing his praises.

But the notion of an exalted *Satguru* always troubled me. This was the early '70s, and the Jesus freaks, "est"-people and followers of myriad *babas* and *anandas* (often themselves former Epsteins and Moskowitzes) had signs and wonders of their own. It was as though there were three types of people in the world: skeptics, those who had found God and those who only thought they had found Him. (And of course, the latter only made it harder for those of us in the middle category to get through to those in the first.)

Nevertheless, I continued to have extraordinary experiences that reinforced my allegiance to the guru. While practicing a meditation technique called "listening to the music," strains of a Renaissance motet wafted ethereally through my right ear! The sound was so vivid, I barely made it through the first stanza before jumping up to make certain no one had a radio on in the adjacent room. (There was no radio; but after the unscheduled intermission, no more motet.)

Another time, I became immersed in something I can only relate to the phrase "filled with the Holy Spirit." I called my wife, Diane, into the little, darkened hallway I used for meditation and tried to describe what I was feeling. But the sensation only quickened, outstripping any thought of running commentary. This time, it seemed right to give the experience my undivided attention, and Diane (assessing me no danger to myself or others) graciously excused me to whatever I was in the throes of.

This meditation had the feel of a tutorial—some precognitive colloquy that rose, as I tuned in, to an inspired height. I exulted there some inchoate while. And then, like the parting kiss of a spiritual lover, my reverie came into more prosaic focus.

I was a public defender by this time, and the upshot was a new perspective on my clients (indigent criminal defendants), on one hand, and those presiding over their due process, on the other. I tried to capture the idea part of this in a poem:

Paragons and Miscreants

Our paragons and miscreants were cut from selfsame cloth.
And equally enfranchised in the only mortal business—
that of getting (or of staying)
just as comfortable as circumstance permits.

By dint of jurisprudence drafted by my well placed peers,
our livelihood seems honest and secure.
My clients, though, must answer
for desires we can satisfy but they can ill afford.

And for us, a nonpecuniary perk:
We're seen all the more upstanding for our salutary work.
Our pride and joy; their due process . . .
All men are berated equal.

Whatever the above evokes, there was no trace of cynicism nor self-reproach in the experience itself. No polemic against lawyers or some power elite, the essence of the epiphany was its very objectivity. Crowning of a bright, nonverbal piece, it was awareness, not thought—a beholding: of the ultimate innocence of every human being, however derelict his behavior.

I'm sure many people can look back on their lives and recall singular moments they felt in touch with the Divine. These may be associated with the early stage of one spiritual path or another. I heard a priest, once, reflecting on the visitations that first called him to the priesthood. Now nearer the end of his vocation, he shared this wise hindsight: "Our spiritual life cannot subsist on exotic visions we may be graced to see or feel. So should you chance upon a burning bush, receive it as a sacramental boon. But then, as Moses did, get on about your Father's work. Lest *un*called for mystic pining obscure, rather than illumine your earthly path."

Lacking all such maturity, I started ranking my meditations. Then, just as fast as enlightenment had struck, I seemed to lose the meditative knack. For a while, I thought this must be some kind of test—why else would God have just stopped showing up? In my youthful ardor, it seemed only reasonable for the extraordinary (now that I'd validated its existence) to consign itself to my meditative beck and call.

Soon enough, though, the press of my own worldly business had me wondering how many hours of meditation a riff of monaural music was really worth. At the risk of getting further ahead of myself, my thought today is, not very many! Perhaps the special effects were provided in the beginning as a kind of spiritual Welcome Wagon. After which I was being called more and more, not less and less . . . to notice the miraculous in my everyday life and interactions.

In time, I made grudging peace with the inconsistency of my meditational experience and took my spiritual pleasures where I found them. For example, I'd been told during my initiation ceremony that if I ever got near enough to Gurudeva Ji, I should cup my right ear and ask him for "holy breath." With that in mind, I positioned myself outside the rear entrance of a hall where the guru was speaking, hoping to catch him on his way out.

"Gurudeva Ji, could I have holy breath?" I petitioned, as he came bounding toward me. The guru grabbed me affectionately around the shoulders. Then, curling the fingers of his other hand to form a tube, he gave a quick blow into my right ear. At that instant, I felt a corkscrew like penetration—not of air but of some unknown medium. It was strangely nonphysical, though it did seem to enter through the ear.

Once again, the sensation was so vivid, it seems pointless to quibble over its reality (whatever I may now make of its significance). Certainly, I'd been "programmed" to expect something cosmic, but what does that really explain? If a faith healer exhorts someone into a suggestible state, does that make the ensuing experience any less real? Looking back with this perspective, I've no good explanation for holy breath (or other phenomena we experienced as devotees of Gurudeva Ji).

Nor for a similar episode with Diane, long before I'd begun testing any spiritual waters. When she first told me she loved me, her *statement* had the same kind of penetrating effect—that time a slicing (not spiraling), into the center of my chest. As with holy breath, it wasn't uncomfortable; just vivid and completely out of the ordinary.

Our young marriage was sorely tested, however, when I became a devotee of Gurudeva Ji. For though I've focused here on a few sensational experiences, it was the subtler but more consistent quality of devotion emanating from the guru's followers (but not my wife) that was winning my spiritual heart.

These were people of all ages, some children and some in their eighties, who would step to the front of the room and express their love for God in the most personal and eloquent ways. There were no agendas, scripts or cue cards for these nightly *satsang** programs. Only those who felt moved to speak came forward, and no one rushed to fill the occasional meditative hiatus.

I found the inspiration and sense of well-being at *satsang* so intoxicating, I soon was taking pains to get there for my nightly fix. Needless to say, our home life was profoundly affected by this dependency . . . and by my absence.

Diane had just completed her masters in social work and taken a job as a family and child therapist. She'd also started into her own psychoanalysis. Her professional and personal lives were thus orienting her 180 degrees from the direction life was taking me.

*Sanskrit for "company of truth" or "holy discourse."

The more blissful I became, the more insufferable she found me. We finally agreed I would take an apartment not far from the *satsang* hall. But our trial separation didn't last long, thanks to another divine intervention.

It was a Sunday morning, and I was at the Sears Auto Center, waiting on an oil change. I passed the time with the *Aquarian Gospel,* a New-Age scripture that was making the rounds of the devotees. But I couldn't concentrate on my reading. Diane and I hadn't spoken for about a week, and my mind kept wandering to that situation. Should I call her? Should I wait for her to make the first move?

I paced a number of times to the pay phone on the wall. Soon, a random but authoritative idea took hold: "READ THE NEXT CHAPTER OF THE BOOK AND THEN DE-CIDE." I sat back down, opened to exactly where I had left off, and this is what I found:

Chapter 77
Jesus in Hebron. Goes to Bethany.
Advises Ruth Regarding Certain
Family Troubles.

* * *

The evening came; the multitudes were gone, and Jesus, Lazarus and his sisters, Martha, Ruth and Mary, were alone. And Ruth was sore distressed. Her home was down in Jericho; her husband was the keeper of an inn; his name was Asher-ben.

Now, Asher was a Pharisee of strictest mien and thought, and he regarded Jesus with disdain.

And when his wife confessed her faith in Christ, he drove her from his home.

But Ruth resisted not; she said, "If Jesus is the Christ, He knows the way, and I am sure he is the Christ."

"My husband may become enraged and slay my human form; he cannot kill the soul, and in the many mansions of my Fatherland, I have a dwelling-place."

*And Ruth told Jesus all; and then she said, "**What shall I do?**"*

And Jesus said: *"Your husband is not willingly at fault; he is devout. He prays to God, our Father-God.*

He feels assured that he has done the will of God in driving you away.

Intolerance is ignorance matured.

The light will come to him someday, and then he will repay for all your heartaches, griefs and tears.

And Ruth, you must not think that you are free from blame.

If you had walked in wisdom's ways and been content to hold your peace, this grief would not have come to you.

It takes a long, long time for light to break into the shell of prejudice, and patience is the lesson you have need to learn.

The constant dropping of the water wears away the hardest stone.

The sweet and holy incense of a godly life will melt intolerance much quicker than the hottest flame or hardest blow."

"Just wait a little time and then go home, with sympathy and love. Talk not of Christ nor of the kingdom of the Holy One.

Just live a godly life, refrain from harshness in your speech, and you will lead your husband to the light."

And it was so. *

Decades later, I can hardly read this text without getting a lump in my throat. Diane was as ensconced as any Pharisee in her psychoanalytic religion. Her concern for my well-being was sincere. But like Ruth's husband, she'd grown intolerant of my heresy.

For those surmising I'd subliminally seized upon the next chapter-heading ("Jesus Advises Ruth, etc.") as a means of resolving my ambivalence about phoning Diane, give at least my grandiosity the benefit of the doubt. Just the synchronicity between my issue and Ruth's would have gone straight to my head, and it was in such a state that I proceeded to call upon Diane.

Whereupon, in total derogation of the pearl cast before me, I heard myself extolling *the guru* once again to my long-suffering wife! Some trance-like *satsang* poured out of me for five, seamless minutes.

Only this time, Diane was taken (not turned off) by the proselytic onslaught. When I finally stopped speaking, she confessed her growing attraction to whatever was so moving me!

*Reprinted by permission of De Vorss Publications, from *The Aquarian Gospel of Jesus the Christ,* by Levi.

I'm reminded here of the restaurant scene in *When Harry Met Sally,* where Meg Ryan fakes an orgasm to prove to Billy Crystal she's not sexually repressed. (A woman at the next table tells the waitress, "I'll have whatever *she's* having.")

So was this all some kind of spiritual masturbation? Was any part of it real? Or was it, like Meg Ryan's performance, an audacious prank? (And if so, *who* was the prankster?)

Diane did let me "lead her to the light," and she too had some memorable experiences as a devotee. But whatever spell Gurudeva Ji and I had cast on her soon began to wear off. As our relationship again deteriorated, that reversal added inexorably to my own growing doubts about the guru.

These had to do with the increasingly unrealistic burden of daily meditation (two hours for serious devotees) and nightly *satsang* of equal length; impromptu devotional gatherings, wherever Deva Ji called them (like the one Cousin Jeff had come all the way from England to attend); and incessant appeals to buy the guru another car, house or helicopter!

Then at *satsang* one evening, they announced that the whole divine enterprise was going out of business. Our erstwhile guru would continue to make public appearances (and presumably to accept donations). But no longer was he on a mission from God. It was time for us devotees, in short, to get a life.

The cosmic pretensions, the entire personality cult had been foisted on young Deva Ji by his now too parochial Indian flock. And, apparently, his own mother . . . at whose urging, back in the old country, the faithful were now flocking to the lotus feet of her more doting son, Megaditto Ji.

Hearing this, I felt called to speak in a manner that was anything but trance-like. "As far as I'm concerned," I declared, "Deva Ji can carry on as *Satguru*—and let the world keep right on calling him a con artist. Or he can retire comfortably . . . and prove the world right! *Satguru* or con artist, he surely doesn't qualify for anything in between."

3

Sarah

My condition in the late '70s and early '80s was one of severe disillusionment, not knowing what to make of the above experiences and trying to limp along without a sense of spiritual direction. I had given up my apprenticeship at the large law firm after only a year to become a deputy public defender for Cook County. Schizophrenic as my professional and devotional responsibilities had made me during that year in private practice, it was impossible even to feign meditative equanimity in the frenzied environment of the Public Defender's Office. So after three hectic years there, I took refuge in a position at Loyola Law School, teaching legal research and writing to first-year students.

At Loyola, I struck up a friendship with a faculty member who, on learning of my spiritual search, confided that he himself had been working with a psychic healer. For a while, I resisted his offer to introduce me to her, but my curiosity soon got the better of me.

Far from the smell of incense and devotional pictures that greeted a visitor to Deva Ji's ashram, Sarah's home and demeanor were quite unassuming. A middle-aged woman (like my Yoga teacher, again Jewish), she lived alone, in a tidy Chicago suburb. But for a few discreetly placed crystals, this could have been the living room I'd grown up in.

After some initial pleasantries, Sarah invited me to lie down on her couch. Standing beside me, she placed the palm of her right hand several inches above my forehead. I felt an immediate ray of focused heat—so much so that I demanded, literally, to have a look up her sleeve.

In many visits with Sarah over the next five years, her psychic gifts were manifest. One time, I mentioned to her that streetlights seemed peculiarly to be going out as I drove by. An hour later, at a nearby restaurant, the ceiling lamp nearest our table expired. The unruly fixture was ten or twenty feet behind Sarah, but when I called it to her attention, she didn't turn around. She merely lowered her head and closed her eyes . . . and that light came right back on!

Fascinated as I was by such displays, our agenda wasn't psychic titillation but spiritual counseling. I continued to assume there was more to life than earning a living, but whatever that might be, I certainly didn't feel connected to it. In the meantime, I could neither recreate nor explain away those intoxicating spiritual episodes I'd credited to Gurudeva Ji.

Sarah thus served as a bridge between my more inspired past and my current workaday life. She assured me that my experiences as a devotee had been real, if perhaps over-rated. She herself had little use for gurus, and certainly no interest in becoming one to me. She charged a modest, hourly fee for our sessions. And like any good counselor, she mostly listened, offering occasional feedback.

But where a therapist might have used my body language or choice of words to gain an understanding of my conflict, Sarah was as likely to comment on what my *aura* was doing as I recounted a particular experience. She'd also pass along tidbits of intuited information, sometimes with attribution to what she called "spirit guides." Their input could be verbal, symbolic, or even psychosomatic.

For example, Sarah might have an acute physical reaction to something I said—a cramped muscle, a cough, an itch, or some other manifestation we'd both try to interpret. At a minimum, these would signal that the symptom-triggering word or theme called for further examination.

One such phrase, at the start of our work together, was "valuable, but not gratifying." I had used it in describing some event that had benefited me professionally, but which I'd not particularly enjoyed. All my adult life, it seemed, I'd been torn between pursuits that were remunerative/practical, on one side of the ledger, and satisfying/uplifting, on the other.

This evoked, for Sarah, two parallel sets of railroad tracks. "It's like you're running powerful but redundant engines, side by side," she commented, "—an awfully inefficient way to get anywhere. Each train hauls its own cargo, your everyday stuff here, some spiritual regalia there, as though one were meat and the other, dairy."*

"But both are taking you to the same place, Adam," she continued. "The tracks are *parallel*, not perpendicular!"

*Under Jewish law, meat and dairy products are strictly segregated.

I did feel sidetracked by those years as a devotee of Gurudeva Ji. Had I been content to remain in the ambitious frame of mind that had served me so well as a law student, I'd have stayed at the prestigious firm that recruited me right out of school. I'd probably be a partner there by now, well on my way to financial security. I was determined not to let my penchant for soul searching further compromise my career. Yet I still longed for what seemed the heightened consciousness of my early days as a devotee.

"Show me what that *looks* like," Sarah interjected. This took me by surprise, and in my disillusioned state, I doubted I could demonstrate what it was like to be "blissed out." Nevertheless, I closed my eyes and began taking the slow, deep breaths that used to catapult me into meditative oblivion. To my further surprise, I quite easily attained the sensation.

"You really do go way out of your body," Sarah commented. "As for the quality or 'hue' you've been pining for, it's called 'purple.'"

"Purple?" I questioned. "What are you *talking* about?"

"Your aura became quite purple as you went into that meditation. There's nothing wrong with that . . . purple's a nice, even a 'high' color."

"But suppose you were a painter, standing before your easel with a palette full of beautiful colors—the entire rainbow. And the only one you chose to paint with was your favorite . . . purple. Don't you see how limiting this would be to you, Adam, as an *artist?*"

"Blue, yellow, red and green will all feel *different* than purple, but they're no less self-expressive. And they'll add immensely to your finished product . . . if you can just incorporate them."

Sarah's words didn't get me high. Nor did they resolve or even address certain psychodynamics that had caused me, all my life, to play the purple/spiritual off against my other "colors." But I'll always cherish the insight she provided that day, which truly cast my conflict in a different light.

In subsequent sessions, we continued to work on my self-limiting notion that life and its activities were either spiritual or practical. And my all-or-nothing attitude about the value of my experiences in either realm.

"How can it be," I persisted, "that 'God' would have bothered to make contact in response to my prayer, only to lead me on a wild goose chase? Never would I have gone down that road with the guru without those special effects —a cosmic meditation here, a set of magical coincidences there. The truth is, I still cherish those experiences. But given the spiritual dead-end to which they've brought me, how can I not now discredit them?"

Sarah went silent. "I'm reluctant to repeat this," she hesitated; "you're not going to like it."

"*Out* with it, Sarah," I demanded.

"Well, what 'he' just said is . . . 'Even a flower . . . needs shit to grow.'"

4

Dor Vador
(Generation to Generation)

The significance of the following incident will become apparent as the story of my marriage unfolds. It occurred before I'd met my wife-to-be or even had a serious romantic relationship.

I was taking a beginning acting course, as part of my general, liberal arts requirements at Purdue. At that stage of my life, I eschewed all emotional self-expression, regarding "feelings" as excuses weak people made for not having their lives together (like mine was). Consistent with that attitude, I conceived of actors as people who recited dialogue, throwing in a hand gesture here and a facial expression there, as necessary to make the scene convincing.

Since I didn't *believe* in feelings, I certainly couldn't see any value in trying to "identify emotionally" (whatever that might mean) with any character I was asked to play. I came into this class expecting simply to memorize and then "enact" (with all appropriate panache) whatever script might be handed me.

Instead, our liberal airhead of an instructor was into improvisation. He wanted me to "dig deep"; to come up with "my own material."

While I waited outside the room, my classmates cooked up a scene to which I would have to respond. All I was told by way of preparation was that I was returning home from work to my wife of several years.

I walked in, on cue, to discover "my wife" in bed with another man. I surveyed the situation momentarily . . . then simply refused to play my assigned part.

It's not that I was taken aback in any moralistic sense by the scene that confronted me. If I'd had a script, I certainly could have read the husband's lines and mustered some theatrical affect. But I lacked all capacity to identify with his predicament and *react* to it. Being so out of touch with my own feelings, I was, in the absence of canned dialogue, at a literal loss for words.

My stunted emotional condition was matched (or compensated for) by the smug assumption that my own carefully scripted life would never subject me to any such experience. No one I married would be capable of such a betrayal. How, then, could I be expected to identify with this pathetic character?

Three decades later, it's clear that my defensive armor simply didn't permit the kind of spontaneity the acting instructor was asking of me. I was one of the last to realize that my entire personality at the time was pre-scripted dialogue.

I have a younger brother, Earl, who seems as cut off from his feelings today as I was at the time of my acting debut. It was in a conversation with him, not too many years ago, that the root of our emotional problem came into bold relief. Thinking myself to have matured substantially by that time, I presumed to offer my brother some feedback on *his* lagging psychological development. "I can't seem to make contact with you," I goaded. "It's like you're 'not home,' emotionally."

Earl deflected the provocation briefly, then retaliated with the following jab of his own: "Don't expect me to *feel* one way or the other *about you*. I can't give you what you want. It's nothing personal; I just do not feel."

I was taken aback by the incisiveness with which my brother thus cut to the chase, both of our interaction and of his psychological predicament. I asked if he'd always been this way, or could he recall ever having had "a feeling"?

Earl answered with hardly a moment's hesitation: "I was about seven. Dad was ranting at Mother, and I was standing there, crying. 'Why is Daddy mad?' I asked. 'It's not Daddy,' she answered, 'it's the alcohol.'"

Earl's retrieval of this incident in response to my query spoke volumes to me. We'd grown up with an alcoholic father and a passive-aggressive mother. Gerald would verbally abuse Abby each night, while she made herself morally superior (and thus "impervious" to the insults). The effect of her pronouncement, "It's not Daddy, it's the alcohol," was to anesthetize my brother, emotionally, by depersonalizing his experience. With one fell swoop, she thus severed emotional effect from behavioral cause.

This may be how all psychological defenses begin. We try to protect those we love by distracting them from the source of their discomfort. But when Earl asked, "Why is Daddy mad?", Daddy truly was angry. Earl found this upsetting, but at least he was in touch with his own resulting turmoil.

From that day forward, however, he stopped allowing his interactions to register emotionally. Psychology calls this "denial." My father had hurt Earl's feelings; my mother had relieved him of them.

Denying or depersonalizing our pain may seem to make sense when, as in the case of seven-year-old Earl, there's really nothing we can do about the external circumstances that are causing it. The problem is, the habit of denial robs us of the ability to enjoy improved relational conditions when they finally arrive. Subconsciously, we continue to experience life as though still confronted with whatever first put our feelings on hold.*

In summary, my siblings and I were taught to depersonalize the most personal of our interactions. Since it made no sense to be angry at an inanimate bottle of alcohol, Mother's implicit advice was to disregard the emotional upheaval we were experiencing. To "tune out" the most dramatic events of our interpersonal lives.

Gerald, in turn, reinforced our denial by waking up stone sober each morning, as though nothing untoward had occurred the night before. This was our positive male role model, strong and handsome; competent and *un*emotional.

Emotion thus came to be equated, in our minds, with the destructive tirades "the alcohol" inflicted on us each evening. The choice seemed either to blame the alcohol (like Mother) or *become* the alcohol (like Father).

---

*And to rationalize this muted (but now inexplicable) discomfort, we make sure to keep a supply of current-time adversity on hand. Psychology calls this the "repetition compulsion."

My way of dealing with my dad's drinking was different than my brother's, however. I was more combative, mouthing off as much as I dared until forced to retreat from the room or the house. I further distracted myself from this adverse home life by becoming an overachiever. I threw myself into the B'nai B'rith Youth Organization, eventually rising to the presidency of a four-state district. Between my organizational life, schoolwork, choir performances and synagogue activities, I kept myself a very busy and well-adjusted looking young man.

By age 16, I was a Goldwater Republican. I went on to read Ayn Rand's *Atlas Shrugged,* with its ideologically impassioned but altogether unemotional heroes. And by the time I reached that acting class at Purdue, I was acting a lot like Michael J. Fox's smug character, Alex P. Keaton, in the television series *Family Ties.*

So how was such a carefully scripted character drawn, only a few years later, to the seemingly intimate and extemporaneous spirituality of my cousin Jeff and his fellow devotees? How did I myself find the capacity, on the very heels of my acting class fiasco, to speak so movingly (and *improvisationally*) about Gurudeva Ji?

What I've come to understand is that these personae, the worldly, ambitious Adam and the spiritual, introspective one, were two sides of the same unemotional coin. Like my father, I could transform myself from an extroverted but tightly controlled presentation into a state of *spiritual* intoxication. In psychological reality, these two stances were more similar than disparate. What they had in common was their detachment from any relational context or emotional self-expression.

What I needed to learn was how to paint the picture of my life with more than just the purple color of passive spirituality (and whatever color my Michael J. Fox persona epitomized). To show my *true* colors—even as they might change from situation to situation. To correct the inconsistency between my outward appearance and what I wasn't allowing myself to feel. To communicate with emotional content, not just audience-pleasing theatrics.

In short, to reengage my interpersonal apparatus. As a complement to whatever intellectual and spiritual acumen I'd begun to develop.

PART TWO

RELATION

Midrash For Part Two:
The Kotzker Rebbe Rides Again*

In the sermon that would prove her swan song, a learned but New-Age rabbi stirred the following pot:

What would we do, my friends, if we were down, God forbid, to our last loaf of bread? Would we bring it here to the Synagogue? Would we hoard it for "our own"?

If this seems a tad dramatic, just reflect on the things we do routinely for survival—"for a living," as we say. How, in other words, do we *get* stuff? Does it come at anyone else's expense? And with whom, when all is said and done, do we *share* our stuff—on what terms?

These may sound like mundane or elementary ethical questions, but I hope to convince you that in actuality, they're the most profound, the most *spiritual* ones we face.

*Rabbi Menachem Mendl of Kotsk, d. 1859, was famous for his uncompromising bluntness. A recluse in his final years, he committed some heretical act that his followers, out of respect for his otherwise exemplary life, refused to elaborate.

To that end, let's begin with a familiar but enigmatic verse from today's Torah reading, *"Uvayom hash'vii, shavat vayinafash*—On the seventh day, God ceased His work and rested." Now this text (Exodus 31:17) expands upon the more concise account at Genesis 2:2, *"Vayishbot bayom hash'vii*—He rested on the seventh day." The words *"shavat"* and *"vayishbot"* (which we translate, "He rested") have the same root—from which, of course, *"Shabbat"* (Sabbath) also derives.

But the additional verb in today's passage, *"vayinafash,"* comes from the root *"nefesh,"* or "soul." This could mean that in His fathomless, Divine Soul, God was deeply moved, or satisfied by what He'd created. Nachmanides* goes so far as to suggest that those who keep the Sabbath are rewarded with an *extra,* or a bonus soul for the day.

But there's another interpretation, perhaps closer to what Nachmanides was getting at. According to a little known *midrash,* the verb *"vayinafash"* can be either transitive or intransitive—intransitive meaning the Divine Essence "ensouled" or individuated Itself; or transitive in the sense that at that instant, God gave *us our* Soul.

Either way, the *midrash* turns a passive, sabbatical moment, one of cessation and replenishment, into an active, seminal one—if you will, the *second* big bang of creation. God becomes at once the Subject and the

*Rabbi Moshe ben Nachman, d. 1270.

Object (the Energy and the Mass) of His own handi-work. In this sense, He doesn't "rest" from His labors so much as He passes the creative torch over *to us.* Or, just as aptly, we pick it up and run with it!

I'm not suggesting God bowed out of the creative process altogether on the seventh day. As we say in the morning prayer, *"Uv'tuvo m'chadeysh b'chol yom tamid maaseh b'reyshit*—In His goodness, He renews daily His physical creation." And as we recite on spe-cial occasions, *"shehecheyanu v'kimanu*—He both fashions and *sustains* us" in our physical parameters.

But I'm going to ask you, now, to think of this world God creates and sustains as but the backdrop for a second wave of creativity—Part Two in His/our ongoing evolutionary process. Picture the whole physical package, the heavens above and the earth below, the world and all that dwell therein, as a kind of spiritual staging ground, a *tabula rasa,* if you will. On which the most generative element, the very stem cell of all our future growth is—and this may surprise you, my friends . . . our physical (individual) *self-interest.* The very thing we bit into, or bit *off,* when Adam and Eve ate from the Tree of Knowledge!

Stay with me here, please—I know this is getting rather complicated. In the cosmology I'm asking you to entertain, God's orderly physical creation becomes Adam and Eve's *"tohu vavohu"* (primordial soup)—a place of material shortage and economic need. From which raw material they will now be charged with re-newing daily the work of . . . *relational* creation!

In the Garden, you see, we were like all the other animals—the top dogs, perhaps; animate, but spiritually half-baked. It was only outside Eden's safe confines, at the synapse between the physical/sensational and the economic/relational, that human life, as we know it, could begin.

And it's at this point, I should give you fair warning, that the *midrash* (and my own theology) take a truly radical turn. For if you follow what I've said so far, what some call our "original sin" now becomes the very fruit of Adam and Eve's ineluctable thrust for relation—a stepping *up,* not a falling down! Yet this enormously important, even courageous step —and here, you see, is the rub—does not sit well in biblical heaven.

*"So you want a **RELATIONSHIP,**"* booms the Lord of Genesis to Eve. "Well, suffer the pain of childbirth—then you'll have something to *relate* to your husband (and all those little ones) about! And you, Adam, will have to clothe and feed them. You may rue the day Eve convinced you there was more to life than guiltless (and unprotected) sex!"

"You say you ate of the forbidden fruit in order to be *like God?* The truth is, you want to *surpass* God. For I, the Lord, **AM ONE**. Now good luck to *both* of you!"

My friends, this angry, vindictive Lord is a creator who has lost His way! In the course of subjectivizing the very objects of His creation, His own objectivity seems to have abandoned Him. Maybe just the thought, the *aspiration* to such indigenous, *intervivos* effect—to the shared risk that's the hallmark, the *sine qua non* of our relational possibilities—proved a slippery slope; some vortex through which His singular Essence (not just His Image), in effect, *eloped.* At once fashioning (transitive) and ripening (intransitive) . . . into *Personhood.*

"VAYINAFASH!"

Whatever the explanation, the Lord of our Scripture was never quite the same. I must speak my truth here, friends—it's getting hard to even capitalize His G! For in a short while, this jealous—let me just call him *'little*-god' for present purposes—repents of his solitude to forge relationship with the Children of Israel. But even as his Higher Self is now courting us with the Ten Commandments, little-god is attaching to them a congenital string: In the event of disobedience, he vows to visit the iniquity of the parents upon the children. And by that pronouncement, you see, *psychology* was born.

Psychology is the impact of our ensuing misbehavior unto the third and fourth generations. We thus become the instruments of little-god's impassioned discipline, inflicting collective punishment on each other. And to our great shame . . . and *this,* my friends, (not our reproductive organs) is the source of that shame . . . on our own offspring.

The therapists call it "displacement." Mom and Dad's original sins are displaced onto our significant others, with whom we continue to act out what are, in reality, generational conflicts. Soon enough, our own children become props in the emotional drama, thereby acquiring their grievances against us.

It took one for sensation, two for relation; and three or four such stiff-necked generations to enmesh ourselves in the neurotic conundrum. Now, added to the problem of how to get things and what to share with whom, we must differentiate between fallout from our current getting, sharing and refusing to share and conflicts that are old (or someone else's).

Only by unraveling this great psychospiritual puzzle (other traditions call it *"karma"*) can we free ourselves and our progeny from a covenant that's in need of renegotiating. For we've been backpedaling since the day Adam and Eve called sensation into the service of latent relation.

Our emotional exile is a vestige of little-god's primordial hurt feelings. We must help him (and ourselves) get *over* it.

5

Tanya and Sherman

By the early '80s, the channelers had largely supplanted the gurus at the vanguard of the New-Age. Their books were on the best seller lists, and Tanya, among others, was crisscrossing the country.

When she came through Chicago, I signed up for one of her public demonstrations. I had run the idea by Sarah, whose own channeled input was, "Adam might find this of interest."

I should say a word about Sarah's type of channeling and how it differed from what I was about to experience. Indeed, Tanya's own alter ego, "Mr. Dillon," once explained it this way:

> This is called "dead trance," where Tanya leaves her body and I come through. Then there's the trance where the person feels the spirit and gives the message, like a psychic reading, which can be good, too.

Sarah fell into the latter category. She herself was fully present while intuiting the message, so it remained her choice whether to pass any or all of it along.

But Tanya claimed to be absent from her body and oblivious to what was being said by Dillon. Theirs was like a landlord-tenant relationship: The body still belonged to Tanya, but for the duration of the trance, Dillon's occupancy was exclusive.

Tanya began the program by explaining the mechanics of trance, as she understood them. The lights were then dimmed, and someone with a guitar began leading us in Bette Midler's "The Rose."

Tanya seated herself and closed her eyes. After a moment, her head slumped forward. We sang on, watching for the smallest telling twitch.

Suddenly, the head jerked back upright and the eyes popped open. The mouth smiled, more on one side than the other. And in a strong, masculine sounding voice, the words "FAITH AND FELICITY BE WITH YE!" rang out.

"Mr. Dillon" now spoke for several minutes on some spiritual theme. I don't remember his specific topic that night, but we were utterly charmed by his "presence." His personality, vocabulary and sense of humor were quite unlike Tanya's. (Indeed, as Dillon was later to point out, most people found it easier to relate to *him* than to Tanya.)

We were enthralled by tales of psychic wizardry at these early trance sessions. A man who had previously asked Dillon about a problem knee reported having awakened, later that same night, in a peculiar position—up on all fours, but with the bad leg extended behind him. And from then on, the knee had given him no further trouble.

He went on to describe a dream in which he thought Dillon had communicated with him. I was seated near the front of the room that evening, up close to Tanya/Dillon. As the man related the dream/message, I could hear Dillon, under his breath (or Tanya's), *anticipating it,* word for word.

By the time Diane and I met Tanya/Dillon, our relationship had again deteriorated, to the point we were barely speaking. In fact, I'd not mentioned the trance circle to her until the last moment and was rather surprised when she asked to come along.

At first, Dillon displayed an uncanny awareness of our personalities and relational gridlock. But then he asked us if we'd like to be married. Diane politely informed him we'd been married for twelve years. "I'm talking about being married *in the spirit,*" Dillon replied. "Would you like to be married *by me?*"

Diane quickly took him up on the offer, her enthusiasm again catching me off guard. For all the distance between us, there'd been no talk of divorce. But neither had I contemplated re-upping, much less for multiple lifetimes. I'll digress here to explain a tenet of Dillon's teaching that was coming into play, though at the time, we were only vaguely aware of it.

He taught that each soul has an "eternal soulmate"—a preordained spouse; a match literally made in heaven. Such couples have a synergistic effect on each other's individual (spiritual) growth. The relational whole is greater than the sum of its parts.

Dillon thus lumped all marriages into one of two categories: "karmic" or "eternal." "Karmic" meant the pair was together to address conflicts left over from a prior lifetime. This was important work, but once the karma was resolved, the relationship had no further *raison d'etre.*

"Eternal soulmates" might have their own conjugal karma to clean up. But in their case, the union would then blossom (not fizzle); lifting them, in the process, to their highest individual potentials.

Diane and I were eventually converted to this vision of marriage, which became the centerpiece of our apprenticeships with Tanya/Dillon (and Tanya's own husband, Sherman). If Gurudeva Ji was to have shown me how to speak to God, they would show the two of us how to approach Him as a relationship.

And how to speak to each other. With guest appearances by Dillon, Tanya and Sherman offered a three-day seminar, billed as a life-changing event for the couple. It was, for the relationship, what *shaktiput* (initiation) was for the individual spiritual seeker.

This was quite different from the spiritual counseling I'd experienced with Sarah. She didn't offer conjoint sessions, nor was she focused on relational issues as such. Indeed, when I raised the eternal soulmate concept during my transition from her tutelage to Tanya and Sherman's, she took exception to it.

Sarah went so far as to suggest that from a psychospiritual point of view, Diane and I were, if anything, a *mismatch*. In all events, she rejected the idea of a preordained "Mr. or Ms. Right," for each person and for all time.

My own experience of our twelve-year marriage cast ample doubt on any notion Diane and I were together "for all time." So (like any prudent lawyer attending his first trance circle) I demanded Dillon's personal assurance that we were, indeed, "eternal soulmates." Only then did I allow him to place his blessing on the relationship.

I don't remember anything out of the ordinary at our nuptials the next day (except that they were being performed by a dead man, speaking through a woman's body). We repeated our vows, exchanged new rings and I kissed the bride.

In addition to these matchmaking services, Dillon offered us individual guidance. With respect to my singing, for instance, he told me the problem was that my throat *chakra** was closed. I asked if he could help me get it *open,* to which he replied:

Well, one way is to tell the truth all the time and live your life in integrity. That, my son, allows for all the gifts of the spirit, which music is, to open up.

But the greatest gift I can give you, Adam, is my sense of humor! To be able to *laugh* as you sing is joyful in God, is it not? So what you have to do is, come, tomorrow, with a song to sing *for me!*

Dillon then asked if we had any instruments, and someone offered up a bass fiddle they'd dubbed "Barbara." Now *Dillon* began to sing:

Big Brown *Babs,* she does it well!
She'll make Adam sing cuz he'll
go to hell if he
doesn't sing!
A-dam . . . A-*dumb!*
You think you're in *court,*
when you *really* need to be
drinkin' *up the port!*

*Yogananda described the *chakras* as "occult cerebrospinal centers," the awakening of which "is the sacred goal of the yogi."

This cracked everyone up but me. "I really *do* want to sing," I persisted, as if the trick was just getting through to Dillon how badly I wanted it. "I've worked at this so many years, trying all the while to maintain some kind of spiritual perspective."

"Oh Gaaaaahhhddd . . . ," Dillon moaned. *"Will* Adam be 'spiritual' *in court?* Tune in next week!" Thus did he humor us through our attachments and obsessions.

I want to turn, however, to what Tanya and Sherman, in their own flesh and blood, had to offer. They'd come to town every several months to conduct what amounted to group therapy sessions, focused largely on our marital relationships. On the weekends in between these visits, the Chicago group would socialize and "process"* together. Although we were all obviously interested in psychic phenomena and spiritual growth, we also spent time just getting to know one another.

Indeed, the trance itself was becoming less the focus of our weekend soirees even when Tanya and Sherman were with us. I began to appreciate Sherman's own intuitive gift, looking more and more to him as a kind of spiritual big brother. And there was always a sense of the psychic present, to guide and inspire any of us as we processed our personal issues and relational conflicts.

During one such session, for example, I'd been unable to get in touch with anything remotely resembling a feeling (as distinguished from a thought) about what was bothering

---

* "Processing" means stepping back from the task or subject at hand to deal with underlying, interpersonal issues.

me. I'd been sitting for some time against a wall, beneath a window. As my frustration mounted, Tanya's ten-year-old daughter, who was playing outside, suddenly slammed the window shut behind me. The physical jolt threw me into an immediate rage.

Tanya reined me in, stating: "My daughter is very psychic. Please don't aim your anger at her." I took this to mean the girl had somehow been guided to slam that window, thus provoking me into contact with the rage I'd been trying all morning to get in touch with. It was as if an emotional boil had been lanced.

But within moments, the anger shifted to an overwhelming sadness. "It's my *father,*" I blurted out, not knowing why I was saying that. This led to a prolonged account of my relationship with my dad, which (though not at all the focus of my earlier process) was now imbued with an emotional substance my previous sharing had entirely lacked.

It's not that I remembered any new facts about our relationship. It's just that my emotions were finally reuniting with their subject matter. I was accessing the pain we'd all known was "in there," but which I'd been unable, until that moment, to *feel.* This reunion of thought and feeling, I've since come to believe, is the beginning of all emotional healing.

For about a year, we continued our weekly get-togethers with the members of this marital support group (and with Tanya and Sherman on about a bimonthly basis). I also continued to visit intermittently with Sarah. In one of those sessions, I told her we'd signed up for Tanya and Sherman's three-day marathon, the "Eternal Marital Relationship Seminar."

On hearing this, Sarah furrowed her brow and expressed concern over what she foresaw for me at the event. "Take plenty of vitamin C," she encouraged, "and try to get a lot of rest; it isn't going to be easy work."

During that same session, she took me through a hypnotic, "past-life regression." I saw myself as a rabbi, married to Diane. Our relationship, as in the present, was a cold one. Diane had done something—I couldn't get the specifics, but it was in the nature of a religious or moral transgression. I'd convened a rabbinic court to address the matter, having made a firm, if painful decision that my wife must be treated no differently than anyone else in the administration of religious law.

Diane never forgave what she considered my excessive show of principle. For the rest of that lifetime together, she was obedient but distant. Just as I'd insisted on the letter of the law, so she now performed her wifely duties to the letter, but entirely without spirit.

At this point, Sarah asked me to envision our last interaction in that lifetime. I saw myself kneeling at Diane's deathbed. I was terribly remorseful of the choice I had made. "If only I could go back and do it differently," I lamented, "I'd make *her* more important than any religious principle."

"Your prayer was heard," Sarah interjected. "The current life is your opportunity to *make* that different choice."

It is difficult to capture my experience of this session—I can't say I felt either deeply hypnotized or vividly aware of the imagery in a pictorial sense. It was more like free association than watching a movie.

Yet I was having an intense emotional response as I described these scenes to Sarah. I *felt* the rabbi's profound grief at the bedside of his dying wife. Whether it was my life or anyone's I was tapping into, some kind of catharsis seemed to be taking place.

Sarah didn't alert me to any connection between all this and the "hard work" we were about to do with Tanya and Sherman. Nor did I tell them anything about the above session with her. But Sherman began prodding Diane, almost from the start of our weekend together, asking if there wasn't something she wanted to get off her chest. And she soon confirmed his intuition . . . that she'd been having an affair.

I was, of course, devastated by this revelation. We spent the next several days filling in every bitter detail—and every other secret my wife had kept from me (or I from her). As Sarah had predicted, this was one of the most stressful emotional experiences of my life.

But through the tumultuous days and weeks that followed, I took consolation in that earlier session with Sarah. The Rabbi's regret—and Sarah's advice to take a different approach this time around—held out a silver lining: the possibility that real growth might result from this catastrophe, depending on how I handled it.

Diane was remorseful, begging my forgiveness. As bad as things were, there was at least a framework in place, under Tanya and Sherman's auspices, for our eventual reconciliation.

Indeed, if they were right about the eternal soulmate concept, perhaps—just perhaps—the wreckage of our marriage could be hauled away and the foundation laid for a different kind of relationship. One in which I might find both the spiritual and the interpersonal substance I'd long been craving.

6

Picking Up the Pieces

The total breakdown of my marriage that came to light in the session with Tanya and Sherman would have forced me to reassess my life and goals even if soul-searching hadn't already become, for me, an avocation. By now, we'd been to mainstream Ph.D. and M.S.W.-type marriage counselors, and Diane had been through psychoanalysis. Nevertheless, and despite the shambles we'd made of our marriage, neither one of us seemed ready to call it a marital day.

Tanya and Sherman, meanwhile, were assuring us that the "healing" of our relationship had already begun. If we wanted to accelerate the process, they and several other couples were forming what amounted to a live-in support group for dysfunctional families. In, of all places, a town called Normal, Illinois.

They described it as a community in which, under Mr. Dillon's ultimate authority, the participants would pursue their individual spiritual development while reconstituting their marriages and family lives. It seemed a unique opportunity to turn our adversity to advantage. With one stroke, we could make a clean physical break from our sordid past and begin a new spiritual adventure.

When Sarah answered the door on my next visit, her greeting was, "Going somewhere? Come in and tell me about it." In spite of some misgivings about Tanya and Sherman, she was respectful of Tanya's psychic gift and never questioned the reality of Mr. Dillon. She also intimated we'd gain much from this experience in the wilds of Central Illinois.

For our families and friends, we tried to make the transition as respectable looking as possible. There were plenty of good reasons to be moving out of Chicago in the spring of 1983. I told my academic colleagues it was time for me to return to private practice, and that I preferred to do so in a smaller-town environment. There was so much crime and traffic in the city. And with the equity we'd accrued in our tiny, three-bedroom house, we'd be able to afford a veritable palace in Normal.

All these things, of course, were true, but beside the point.

Like us, the other couples moving to Tanya and Sherman's community were struggling, to one degree or another, to hold their marriages together. About half (including Sherman) were Jewish. There were two other lawyers and two other psychiatric social workers. We also had a psychology professor, a med-school professor and a dentist. Along with our collective emotional baggage, we shared an egalitarian vision of communal living and psychological self-help.

We purchased five large houses in a nice residential neighborhood. We developed a home-schooling program for the children. The idea was to create a self-contained community, in which our kids would be surrounded by a nurturing, extended family. We'd all feel welcome in any of the five households. And we'd be knowledgeable of and engaged in each other's personal and familial processes.

To that end, but also for economic reasons, we lived two to three families per house. For while some of us had arrived with money in the bank, the group included waiters, delivery-people, construction workers . . . and lots of kids. As a result, our mission to save our marriages came also to entail forging community, under these emotionally dire but adventuresome circumstances, across social and economic lines. Just as husbands and wives were recommitting to each other as eternal soulmates, our families were undertaking to share all aspects of the communal burden—social, psychological, spiritual and economic.

Neither Diane nor I had ever been involved in anything so radical. But we were doing this together. We were once again on the same team. And we believed we were finally turning our dysfunctional relationship into something truly noble.

As I recall these early, halcyon days in the community, I'm still struck by our bold idealism. Here we were, eventually forty or so adults, many of us professionally, if not interpersonally accomplished; committing ourselves and our resources to a common vision of marital and communal life that we were learning and inventing as we went along.

We were going to help each other uproot all vestiges of selfishness, pride, deceitfulness and self-suppression. We'd work diligently, within each relationship and household, to handle every interpersonal conflict (and all the practical challenges of daily living) at the inspired level we'd experienced during our weekend sessions with Tanya and Sherman.

And for the first year or so—while we were able to live off our savings—the experience was truly exhilarating.

7

Energy

I've just returned from a lecture by Rabbi and author Joseph Telushkin, who previewed his new book, *Words That Hurt; Words That Heal*. Telushkin's topic was "the ethics, not the psychology" of human communication. He calls for the creation of a national day on which we'll all refrain from uttering even a single harsh or hurtful word.

As I'll attempt to explain below, the Rabbi's focus on our verbal output (rather than the more elusive psychology and spirit of the interaction) is just the opposite of what we were striving for in the community. We believed that the integrity of our communication, certainly in the husband-wife context, demanded emotional authenticity at all times. We therefore focused not on the words *per se,* but on the internal conflicts and relational issues that were animating our hurtful speech.

While my view of this has moderated in the intervening years, I still believe great and small harm is routinely inflicted by "appropriate" words, whose effect, like odorless carbon monoxide, is nonetheless toxic. Unless and until the underlying emotionality is addressed, it continues to impact our loved ones, whether we soften the verbal blows or censor them entirely.

As though anticipating the above, the Rabbi reminded his audience that our first duty is to behave decently, however we may be feeling on the inside. Better to feed the hungry, even with resentment, than to hold out, at their expense, for some psychospiritual epiphany. The fundamental precept of *tzedaka* (righteousness) commands us to relieve what suffering we can; and strive for a more loving spirit (*kavana*) as we go along.

Judaism thus assigns a higher value to *tikun olam* ("repair of the world") than to personal growth (or, for that matter, salvation). One's speech, Telushkin argues, is no less subject to this behavioral mandate. Until we can rise above our hurtful sentiments, we should find the self-control to muzzle them . . . at least for one day out of the year.

Of course, true *tzaddikim* (righteous ones) have managed to combine the letter with the spirit of the law. These great souls are exalted in Jewish literature and storytelling. In Buber's *Tales of the Chasidim,* he recounts a disciple of one such *tzaddik* proclaiming, "I didn't go to the [Master] in order to hear Torah from him but to see how he unlaces his felt shoes and laces them up again." This reminds me of a statement by Ralph Waldo Emerson: "I and mine do not teach by argument, but by our presence."

In the psychological world, a similar debate has raged between the behaviorists (and more recently, the pharmaceuticals), on one side, and the psychoanalysts/talk-therapists, on the other. The former say, "Enough plumbing of the subconscious depths; let's clean up this patient's act!" The latter say, "Give us a few more years of treatment and we'll surely get to the root of the problem. We can then effect a cure, instead of just masking the symptoms."

It wasn't 'til I arrived at Tanya and Sherman's community that I glimpsed the possibility of integrating, in a single framework, the behavioral aspect (words and deeds) with the psychospiritual processes from which our conduct emanates. That would address a concern Diane had raised at the beginning of my spiritual search: that "spirituality" was no substitute for basic psychological (behavioral) health. But going well beyond Telushkin's prescription, our goal was to become conscious of (and take responsibility for) not just our choice of words, but our unspoken attitudes and agendas.

It was on this level that Tanya and Sherman perceived the real spiritual and communicative challenges to lie. They used the term "energy" to capture the silent but trenchant influence Emerson called our "presence." And they had a remarkable gift for seeing the energetic forest through the behavioral trees.

To the less perceptive, this sometimes made their own behavior seem inappropriate or disproportionate. For example, on a visit to Normal before we'd decided to move there, we walked in on a heated argument between Tanya and another member of the group. Tanya became self-conscious—conflicted over whether to sweep the altercation under the rug in deference to the out-of-town guests. (She was well aware that to us, her remonstrations looked unseemly, if not hysterical.)

But Tanya's vehemence reflected her and the community's commitment to "call the energy," i.e., not to sit on unexpressed emotionality. They saw disrespect not in the forceful and direct exchange of angry words, but in disingenuous chatter between people who were energetically pummeling one another. Indeed, that kind of socially appropriate non-communication was as offensive to them as a torrent of cuss words would have been to us.

Tanya did interrupt her tirade long enough to explain that this kind of exchange was normal for them and that we needn't be alarmed. I professed great "cool" about the chaos we'd intruded upon (though, of course, I was politely lying through my teeth).

When things eventually calmed down, Tanya elaborated that the community's way was to respond "cleanly" but uninhibitedly to the energy of the moment. Just as soon as that energy "shifted," it would be as though the conflict had never existed. For once the energy (not just the rhetoric) had truly changed, there would literally be no grudge left to hold.

As I acclimated myself to this no-holds-barred way of interacting, I found it much more alive and honest than what passes for communication in the more polite company to which we were accustomed. I also came to agree with Tanya that our conflicts never really dissipate until fully and cleanly addressed. The devil, of course, is in the details. But the development of our attunement to energy, sufficiently to recognize when it was "off" (in conflict) and when it had shifted (resolution), would be a large part of our work over the next three years in Normal.

I'm sure many psychically gifted people can actually "see" this energy shift, perhaps as a change in the person's aura. Any good therapist uses his own intuitive faculties to recognize when a moment of emotional reality breaks through the chatter of ordinary, defensive banter; when the defenses have been sufficiently penetrated to allow both the consciousness and the behavior to truly change. Whether we speak in psychological or psychic terms, the process is the same. The person finally "gets" (realizes) that small piece of his life's puzzle, and the air is somehow, almost miraculously, cleared.

This differentiation between words and their underlying energy did not come easy to me, however. Indeed, I dismissed it, at first, as so much New-Age psychobabble. Not surprisingly, this created tension between me and the group, which soon accused me of concealing my own hostility behind lawyer-like words and convincing arguments. For an excruciating time, I really had no clue what these people were talking about.

An early incident will illustrate how out of touch I was. Just days after we'd moved to Normal, several of us were kibitzing about the great things we were going to accomplish together. Some comment I made evoked, from Sherman, a slightly teasing but affectionate response: "Oh, am I such a heavy *burden* to you, Adam?"

"You're no burden," I deadpanned . . . "just *fat.*"

Sherman stood up slowly and left the room. A hush fell over the rest of us but didn't last long. Tanya came flying in . . . and ordered me to leave the house!

I left, shaken, apologetic and profoundly confused. Word soon came that I was not to further darken Sherman and Tanya's door "until my energy had shifted." In the meantime, all communication with them was to be through third parties.

I'll not address here the disproportionality of this response to my provocative quip—or the communal power structure it revealed. What I want to focus on, for the present, is the reality of the energetic body blow I had, in fact, delivered to Sherman. And what he and Tanya had to teach me about energy.

Whatever had prompted me to take that little shot, it was my method—the sarcastic, verbal sneak attack—that particularly drew Sherman's ire. For days, I denied any hostile intent. Unfortunately, these people only took "I'm sorry if what I said hurt you" as rubbing further salt in Sherman's wound. The energy remained to be dealt with until I not only admitted but "got" my subjective (if still unconscious*) ill will.

How often do we experience well-meaning apologies that fail to inspire any confidence the offending behavior won't soon be repeated? This isn't necessarily because the apology is insincere. It's because the energy, as distinguished from the behavior, hasn't been identified, much less corrected. Thus, until I could acknowledge my hostility toward Sherman, any regret I might express could only be

---

*However paradoxical, the realization that our behavior is no less intentional when it *is* unconscious was a personal breakthrough, for which I'll always be indebted to Tanya and Sherman.

for the adversity *I* had suffered as a result. (The hostility, meanwhile, would lie in wait for another opportunity to ambush him . . . or someone else.)

Now even as thick as I was in the spring of 1983, I could hardly deny that my sarcastic remark about Sherman's weight was tactless. After some soul searching, I "got" that it was a tad provocative. But the entire fabric of my self-image balked at any notion of actual malice. (Had my mother been there, *she'd* have spoken up for me: "Oh, Sherman, you're making a mountain out of a molehill. You're too sensitive!")

But something Sherman had said, just before leaving the room, stayed with me. Giving no hint of the ax that was about to fall, he'd muttered something about a "feminine energy." Then, standing and with more conviction, he declared: *"That* was a woman!*"* Which utterance evoked, for me, not my mother's but my *sister's* inflection, each time I replayed the tape of what had just slipped out of me.

A psychologist, looking back with me on this incident, might have probed his way to the association between my behavior on this occasion and my sister. The sudden, verbal jab was her trademark in our nightly skirmishes with "the alcohol." But Sherman's insight was spontaneous, not psychological. He didn't deduce my sister's influence; he *felt* it.

Of course, it was my energy (not my sister's) that assaulted him. But the linkage to her soon brought me around to the more pertinent question: What was *I* now lashing out against?

If all this seems too complicated, paranormal or far-fetched, we could just say I'd learned a style of fighting from my sister that I'd unleashed on Sherman, for reasons I did not yet understand. We all borrow in this way from our siblings and parents to perpetuate our distinctive, family brands of what Rabbi Telushkin calls "hurtful speech." But to the extent I might attempt to pass the responsibility off to my sister or mother, they (or their therapists) could just as easily refer us further up the ancestral chain.

Every such familial legacy awaits a generation with the fortitude to say, "Enough is enough. The neurotic buck stops here. I (and my children) shall be free of this."*

I do believe my personal growth, and my children's, was thus accelerated because Tanya and Sherman did for me what no proper therapist would have agreed to do. They subjected themselves, in the relatively unprotected framework of this "spiritual community," to the unfiltered onslaught of my displacement, along with everyone else's.

Experienced therapists know that their patients' transference** can and will exploit any weakness in their professional armor. That's another reason they don't invite the patient home for tea, much less move him into the spare

---

*This should not be confused with the defiant energy psychology calls a "reaction formation" (where we make a point of doing just the opposite of what our parent(s) would have done or wanted). That behavioral strategy only reinforces the emotional legacy from which we think we're distancing ourselves.

**The patient/client's tendency to displace his unresolved parental conflicts onto the therapist.

bedroom, as Tanya and Sherman were doing. They don't share their own hopes, fears and frustrations, lest the patient find a way to use that information against them (or to otherwise sabotage the treatment).

Tanya eventually explained that just moments before my crack about Sherman's weight, he'd confided to her his increasing self-consciousness on that very score. Now Sherman wasn't obese, and it hadn't entered my conscious mind that he was sensitive about his weight. But that doesn't mean I didn't *intuit* the sensitivity.

Sherman and I were thus equally psychic: I by knowing where he was vulnerable; he by sensing my cheap shot had something to do with how the women in my life had influenced me. I doubt any therapist could have gotten the ball rolling more quickly.

In a nutshell, the concept of energy, as taught by Tanya and Sherman, meant we owed a duty, at least to those we claimed to love, to become more fully *conscious*. To take responsibility, not just for our words and behavior, but for the effect our very presence is having on those around us.

Based on this high standard, the community served as an extension of the eternal soulmate relationship. Indeed, we began to speak less of "community" and more of "spiritual family." The idea, or ideal, was to project the same communicative integrity outward, from our nuclear family, on through our extended one. And eventually, even to the stranger on the street.

That, we felt, would be the beginning of real *tikun olam*.

8

Spiritual Community

What roles, then, were we playing for each other in this unusual psychospiritual enclave? We weren't "friends," in the normal sense of that word. There was a definite hierarchy, with Mr. Dillon presumably at the top and Tanya and Sherman taking care of the day-to-day administration of the collective energy. There were also designated "heads of household," who were the initial arbiters of what was going on among the residents of each house.

The organizational structure and spiritual aliveness reminded me of the Children of Israel, on their departure from Egypt. We believed we'd left the bondage of our moribund relationships and psychic ignorance in Chicago, Denver, Philadelphia or wherever we'd come from. We looked to Tanya and Sherman to guide us through the uncharted relational wilderness. And we trusted that an unseen, higher authority would intervene were we to lose our collective, intuitive way.

As suggested above, the commitment to the eternal soulmate was the covenant upon which the social and philosophical structure of the community rested. The marital relationship was seen as both the context and the catalyst for the psychospiritual growth of the individual (and of the group as a whole). We continued to draw inspiration from Tanya's weekly trance, but it was in the small and large conflicts and energy shifts to which the grist of daily living subjected us that we waited on the Lord.

Our lives were thus filled with myriad small moments of interpersonal truth. Our psychospiritual classroom was the kitchen, the work place, the bedroom—wherever we found ourselves. We made no distinction between neurotic, relational and spiritual issues, believing any of these, if examined with courage and determination, would lead us to the Truth. We likewise assumed that our familial and communal conflicts, if handled with integrity, would bring to light and help resolve our most deep-seated individual pathologies.

9

The Eternal Soulmate Relationship: "It Guards Your Breath As It Cleans Your Teeth"

Early in our marriage, we knew a couple who could have been Mr. and Mrs. Jack Sprat. He was thin as a rail, and she was grossly obese. She eventually underwent a surgical procedure to remove part of her small intestine. The purpose of the operation was to allow food to pass more quickly through her system, which would somehow cause her to lose weight.

The operation was a success, but the relationship died. She dropped over 100 pounds; then he dropped her!

It seems self-evident that any significant change in the individual is going to impact the relationship. Is it not incongruous, then, for marriage counseling and individual treatment to be administered as separate disciplines? The therapist treats the individual without input from the absent, but no less impacted spouse; while the marriage counselor addresses the couple's communication, but with scant attention to root psychological issues.

We were thus enthused about combining the work of the therapist and the marriage counselor in a single venue. We believed if we were to make real and lasting progress as a couple, it would be necessary to identify and address the individual neuroses that were driving the relationship. At the same time, we felt that our individual issues were best accessed through the relationship (since that's where they most pervasively presented). And finally, we'd accepted the premise that the marital relationship (with the eternal soulmate gloss added) provided not just the arena but the spiritual catalyst through which the individuals would achieve their emotional healing.

Healing the Relationship: The Medium Is the Message

What is the goal of psychotherapy? Unlike other forms of education, its highly personal curriculum aims specifically at self-knowledge. Nor is it merely an intellectual study. Our increasing self-awareness marks our progress toward emotional and spiritual maturity.

But just as our psychospiritual deficiencies reveal themselves in our behavior, shouldn't individual growth manifest in improved behavior and relationships? For what good is self-awareness if it doesn't help our relationships work better?

I'm reminded here of a conversation, some twenty years ago, with a med student friend who was planning to become a psychiatrist. This young man had a surprisingly cynical attitude about his future career. He frankly stated that his own therapy "didn't work."

"What it achieved," he said, "was the identification of my emotional issues, but without any real impact on them or their relational consequences." His demoralizing conclusion was that we neither feel nor behave better after therapy; we simply earn the dubious privilege of knowing just what we're *doing* to our loved ones and ourselves!

Under the eternal soulmate rubric, by contrast, our vision of emotional health was entirely functional. The relationship served as our psychological proving ground.

But what does "work better" *mean* in the marital context? Many couples are content not to rock the boat—to maintain the emotional homeostasis that attracted them to each other in the first place. Indeed, zeroing in on the energies fueling our conflicts tended, if anything, to *de*stabilize the relationships as presently constituted.

Our idea of improved communication thus wasn't the avoidance of overt conflict at the cost of keeping it covert. In that sense, we saw marital friction as the coin of the therapeutic realm—not to be short-changed into tidy but less evocative "I-statements."

We also knew that whoever's behavior had "started it" on this occasion, there were always reciprocal issues at play—some emotional counterpart in the spouse that made him willing to engage in the drama in the first place. This fight wouldn't be happening—this couple wouldn't *be together*—if their neuroses weren't somehow complementing one another.

We realized, in short, that what defense mechanisms are to the individual, the relational status quo is to the couple. Just as we deny our internal conflicts in a vain attempt to preserve our personal comfort, so the relationship constructs an interlocking network of defenses, looking thereto for some modicum of stability. But as the effect of denial is to cut the individual off from his feelings, so the neurotic symbiosis erodes the couple's capacity for intimacy.

We also recognized that all marital conflict is at once a symptom of and a railing against this very symbiosis. When an argument erupted, we saw it as one or the other spouse's thrust (however unconscious) for *greater* intimacy—a conjoint version of the repetition compulsion. The first step was to identify which partner was thus stirring the neurotic pot on this conflictual occasion.

Our purpose wasn't to referee the conflict or declare one side "right" and the other "wrong." The object was to identify the person who was, in reality, using the conflict to call attention to his own (individual) issue. As we would put it, that person's energy was "up."

The Eternal Soulmate's Carrot

We believed, with all the fervor of religious acolytes, that each partner had both the capacity and the spiritual duty to help heal the other. We reasoned that the spouse could do two things the therapist could not: He could *love* the "patient"; and be there for the long haul.

I've always had an issue with Carl Rogers' claim of "unconditional positive regard" for his clients. How can this be when the very regard is metered out in 45-minute increments, going for $200 per dose? I don't begrudge the therapist his livelihood, but "unconditional" his regard is not.

We, on the other hand, had vowed to love each other "for richer or for poorer, in sickness and in health." As eternal soulmates, we now sweetened the package with a mental health benefit: By communicating ever more cleanly, ever less defensively, we would love our way to the bottom of every conflict; unraveling and dissipating, in the process, wounds and grievances from our distant, individual pasts.

The Eternal Soulmate's Stick

But we also saw the marriage contract as a license to call (confront) the energy whenever we sensed something (behavioral or *pre*-behavioral) disturbing our own equilibrium. As the one who bore the brunt of our partner's neurotic habit, we considered it both our right and our duty to initiate process. In sharp contrast to the therapist's more passive objectivity, our job was precisely to personalize every marital interaction; to insist our spouse take notice of her energy's impact *on us*. To thereby make our presence—and through it, every latent (individual) conflict—truly felt.

That meant never hesitating to probe our partner's defenses in order to give our love the chance to do its healing work. As suggested above, we saw this as the growth-spurring ingredient that was missing from the professional therapeutic relationship.

Of course, doing this cleanly, i.e., knowing *whose* defenses were actually asserting themselves on any given occasion, was much easier said than done. For in establishing the relational homeostasis, we'd learned precisely how to push each other's neurotic hot-buttons. Our mission—to express more love and less pathology—thus became, by definition, an ongoing exercise in self-examination.

It was in this way that the individual and relational processes truly catalyzed one another. For we were determined to do more than just identify our neuroses. We were going to grow ourselves *and* the relationship. Or move on to find the one with whom we might realize such individual and relational synergy.

10

Sexual Awareness

A passage in the Talmud reads, *"Da lifney mi ata omeyd"*— "Know (be aware) before Whom you are standing." This text often appears in the synagogue, on or near the Ark. The concept is that we should live our lives as though always standing before the Holy Ark—knowing that our every act and thought are fully open to God's view.

It was on our initial visit to the community that I was confronted with the practical implications of standing not before God, but before someone with a paranormally intimate view of me. "Take your filthy hands off my daughter and *keep* them off!" Tanya upbraided me.

Now I hadn't physically touched Tanya's attractive teen-age daughter but was as guilty as Jimmy Carter of the lustful thought. This rebuke was my notice Tanya ran a tight ship when it came to sexual energy in particular. Since most of us were used to giving our fantasies free rein, her psychic sensitivity on this score made us nervous and kept us vigilant.

The realization that our sexuality could be observed, even in the absence of the slightest verbal or behavioral "come on," cast a whole new light on our social mores. We began to notice how much sexual communication takes place long before rising to the level of suggestive speech or body language. Our liberated culture has gone almost completely unconscious in this regard. As Dillon used to put it, the same man who might shoot you for touching his car has no problem at all when you dance cheek to cheek with his wife!

But Tanya's zero tolerance for energetic smut was practical, not prudish. Considering the level to which we were holding each other accountable, we could hardly have overlooked foreign sexual incursions into the eternal soulmate relationship. It would have been the height of duplicity to ask another member of the group to process with me—to lower his emotional guard—while I was entertaining sexual fantasies about his wife!

Or to be having sex with my own wife while thinking about someone else's. Indeed, we considered it the spouse's job to ferret out any such energetic philandering. If my partner didn't care where my consciousness was (so long as my sex organ was present and accounted for), *both* of us were being energetically unfaithful.

For our goal was to stop using anyone, from the total stranger to our own spouse, as a sex object. In the case of the spouse, that might mean initiating process even at the cost of *coitus interruptus*. In the case of the attractive stranger, it meant visualizing her mother and father, standing beside her.

"Da," they'd be saying if I would only hear them. "Know before Whom you are standing."

11

Group Psychoanalysis

Diane's experience in psychoanalysis made the consolidation of individual, conjoint and group modalities all the more attractive to us. I'll digress here to describe the psychoanalytic model of emotional healing, as I've come to understand it.

The analyst (usually an M.D. psychiatrist) "treats" the patient in an interpersonally sanitized, clinical environment. Lying on a couch, the patient free-associates (says whatever comes to mind), with a minimum of direction from the analyst. The idea is for the patient, over time, to get in touch with his innermost fantasies and preoccupations.

The analyst, by contrast, remains scrupulously *im*personal in these sessions. Seated behind the patient, like an invisible alter ego, he offers sporadic interpretive comments, the substance and timing of which are what make the process a therapeutic one. But like any good clinician, the analyst monitors the patient's process from a personal/relational remove.

There's good reason for this professional detachment. The symptomatology of the patient's "illness" is his history of unsatisfactory interactions with family, friends, employers, etc. However well handled the analyst's own issues and relationships might be, were he to allow his emotional field to intersect the patient's, he'd become part of the very subject matter he was trying to help sort out.

To prevent this, the analyst takes pains to avoid contact with the patient outside their formal sessions. He likewise cordons himself off from the patient's family and friends, in order to maintain complete confidentiality (and undivided loyalty).

The analytic hour thus amounts to an interactive time out for the patient, a freeze-framing of emotionally charged events for review and interpretation with the analyst before pushing the relational resume-play button. To that end, *both* participants are sequestered from their respective personal contexts for a most private but relationally sterile *tete à tete*.

Now I didn't know any of the above when Diane started her psychoanalysis. However, all the signals my wife was sending suggested that the treatment wasn't going well. Over a period of months, she became increasingly depressed, to the point she was talking (albeit abstractly) of *suicide.* When this got me concerned enough to begin hiding away my razor blades, I took it upon myself to phone her analyst.

Dr. Heinrich spoke to me in terms even a psychologically illiterate young lawyer would comprehend: "Sir, you and I do not have a contract. My contract is with your wife. I cannot discuss this matter with you. So please don't interfere further in my work with Diane."

Even with my current understanding of the importance of confidentiality in the psychotherapeutic relationship, this response to my legitimate, if unsolicited concern strikes me as doctrinaire and overzealous. In all events, the above may shed further light on the appeal Tanya and Sherman's approach had for both of us.

In their community, there was no turf war between the individual and relational processes. The relationship was seen as the very portal to the psychodynamics of the individual. Whatever issues needed to be addressed, it was within the relationship that they would inevitably present. We could then work backwards—from the patent, marital conflicts to the more latent, individual ones.

Tanya and Sherman were thus taking a systems approach, examining the individual issues in their larger, relational context. But they also had on the spot access to the relationship and its constituents. If a conflict erupted at midnight, we'd all roll out of bed and lend our collective insight to its resolution. And we'd stay with the process until the individual energies at play were identified and had shifted.

Needless to say, this created quite a different culture from the one we'd all grown up with. In normal married life, husbands and wives attempt to address their conflicts, if at all, in private. So long as the marital *behavior* remains within bounds, the relationship muddles through its ups and downs, maintaining discretion when on public display.

An unfinished argument on Saturday afternoon thus gives way to convivial chitchat as the dinner guests arrive. Unless and until the pair can no longer keep the lid on, they'll endure this marital schizophrenia, relating to each other one way when they're alone and quite another (like a set of dress clothes) for public consumption.

In the community, we came to disparage the latter as "performance behavior." Our goal was to walk our domestic talk; to live up to the authenticity we espoused, not just at home, but in our social and even economic contexts.

But we didn't do much socializing outside our circle. And economically, we were resting on our collective, if fast dwindling laurels. In short, we'd retreated from the very settings that tend to call for performance behavior in the first place.

In the vernacular of personal boundaries, we had all but erased them among ourselves but erected a firm, parochial one between us and the world at large. Like provoked bees, we'd swarm in at the first sign of non-communicative backsliding within our ranks. (We considered this a form of communal "tough love.") But in the larger scheme of things, we'd severed the umbilical cord of socioeconomic accountability that makes life on earth what it is.

I recall one time we did venture out into the real world. Through an acquaintance on the faculty at Purdue, Diane and I were invited to lead a ten-week pilot program of group therapy for couples. This was under the auspices of the University's Center for Family Studies. The project went so well, several of the couples wanted to keep working with us after the formal program had ended. So we started seeing them at our home, on a weekly basis.

Unfortunately, one of the true zealots of the community took a reading of our energy and concluded we were becoming uppity in our new roles. Our home office was a room that served, when we weren't meeting with the outsiders, as passageway to the laundry room. Unwilling to be inconvenienced by the airs she perceived us to be putting on, this woman came barging through one of our sessions with her basket of dirty underwear (giving a whole new meaning to "airing our dirty linens").

We should have realized then that the gap between the community's uncompromising agenda and the demands of life in the real world was too great to bridge. That authenticity and discretion aren't mutually exclusive; personal boundaries not an all-or-nothing proposition. And that communication can be both honest and sincere without being unrelentingly self-revealing or conflictual.

12

Ego

At one introductory trance circle, a young woman asked Dillon if he could help her become a famous photographer. "You're already famous with me," Dillon quipped; "I don't know what more I could possibly do for you in the 'fame' department."

Dillon never encouraged our thrust for personal status, much less fame. He posited "ego"* as our spiritual nemesis and exhorted us to "overcome" it.

I was thinking about this one day as I waited at the Department of Motor Vehicles to renew my license. After twenty minutes in line, I got close enough to the counter to read that the renewal fee had gone up from $4 to $7. I had $6 in my pocket . . . and my checkbook. But the sign also announced that they'd stopped taking checks.

It was a hot, summer day, and I was tired and fed up. The last thing I wanted to do was drive all the way home and back, just to wait another twenty minutes in line. In my prior, more dignified life, there would have been no alternative.

*I use the term (as did Dillon) in the colloquial, not the Freudian sense.

But my ruminations about ego now ripened into a bold, if unconventional action plan: Why not ask one of the fifty other patrons in line if they'd save me an hour's time by lending me the dollar I was short. (I would mail it back to them or, if they preferred, write them a personal check.)

The thought of doing this threw me into immediate agitation and embarrassment. Was my resistance to so practical a solution something I should endeavor to "overcome"? I turned to the person behind me and simply described my predicament.

A woman standing distinctly off to the side quickly pulled a dollar from her purse, rushed over and handed it to me. When I began to write her a check, she put up her hand, stating: *"I have been told* that I should give you this money—that it's important. Under the circumstances, it wouldn't be right for me to accept your check."

Now it could just be that a disproportionate percentage of Normal's population *isn't*. But I preferred to take meaning from what had just transpired: that Dillon (or some other privy to my internal process) had gotten the attention of my flesh and blood benefactor. Who, in turn, was willing to underwrite a buck's worth of my spiritual education.

More was accomplished here, in my estimation, than the avoidance of a drive home to get the extra dollar.

13

"The Universe Will Provide"
(and Other Euphemisms of Denial)

Experiences such as the above convinced me that virtually any interaction could serve either to dilute or to reinforce my identification with ego. When I hid my distress from those who hurt me, I chose defensiveness over honest communication. When I allowed the fear of rejection to deter me from asking for help, I fostered ego at the expense of relationship and faith in God.

But this seemed a slippery slope. Was there not a line to be drawn between faith and humility, on one hand, and slothful dependency, on the other? Otherwise, what kept us all (in the name of "trusting the process") from just plunking ourselves down in some comfortable spot—with a sign reading, "Vulnerable. Need Cash. God Bless"?

We did that for a while, in a manner of speaking. It wasn't as if we hadn't put our own, hard-earned money where our spiritual mouths were. But somewhere along the way, we lost sight of the fact that neither our marriages nor our spirituality existed in a physical (or fiscal) vacuum. Compounding the error, as our cash and credit resources dwindled over months of non-remunerative interpersonal process, we became self-righteous about our very willingness to turn to others for help.

I remember, for instance, a conversation with a fellow who'd attended a number of the early Chicago trance circles. Brian had stopped short of moving with us to Normal but lent $5,000 to Ed and Jessica to help them make the move. Now, reasonably enough, he wanted to be paid back. And since the debtors were living in my house, it fell to me, as head of household, to monitor the financial and interpersonal heat we were starting to get.

So on Brian's next visit to Normal, I arranged a sit-down for the four of us. He opened the discussion with a rendition of his new mantra, "a contract is a contract." We, of course, weren't interested in the law of contracts, but in the deeper energies at play.

I told Brian there were two ways we could approach this conversation. "Contractually speaking," the debtors had an obligation to repay the money, and he had every right to collect it. But here in Normal, Ed, Jessica, Diane and I had moved beyond obligation (who owes what to whom) to a more personal (if all but unenforceable) way of relating.

The closing pitch went something like this:

> We can sign an ironclad agreement to pay you so much per month, for so many months. If we don't live up to the terms, you can get back in line with our other creditors . . . or file your lawsuit.

> Or we can give you the kind of commitment we've made to each other. The essence of which is, we're accountable [another spiritual term of art] for what we do each day and how we disburse the financial fruits

thereof. Were you to become part of that ongoing discussion, we'd owe you a real voice in our deliberations, financial and otherwise.

I'd be willing to speak to you not just on the monthly basis we deal with our creditors, but daily. I'd welcome you into our soul searching as to which financial need is most compelling at any given moment. By engaging with us in that process, you might get paid back sooner or you might get paid back later than if we go the route of contractual obligation.

The difference is that accountability addresses all our needs and resources (yours included). But under the obligation scenario, the $5,000 Ed and Jessica owe you will delimit your relationship with them . . . and with the rest of us.

The upshot was, Brian agreed to be our brother rather than our creditor.

Yet I was also willing to play the patsy of my own spiritual fast-talk. There was the time Tony and Lisa were living in our house, with their three-year-old daughter and another child on the way. Tony had just gotten a job at the post office, sorting mail on the graveyard shift. I'd encouraged him to apply for that job; in fact, I'd put up the money for the course that got him through the qualifying exam. (And for the new tricycle his little girl had her heart set on for Christmas.)

But at dinner one cold January evening, Tony shared with us how much he hated the new job. He threw in that his coworkers were plying him with amphetamines, just to get him through the nightly shift.

Now I'd known this young man since moving to the community and did feel a sense of commitment to him and his family. But it was our mortgage, not theirs, inching closer to foreclosure. So what I felt like saying was:

YOUR JOB SATISFACTION'S NOT MY PROBLEM. *LIFE'S A BITCH!* NOW **STRAIGHTEN UP AND FLY RIGHT**. And I'd better see your family's share of our expenses without fail on the 15th!

But before I could get that out, I happened to glance at his little girl, playing serenely on the floor with our own toddler-son. Those two were inseparable. I couldn't help but imagine the turn *her* life might take were her daddy to get hooked on speed.

"To hell with that job," I heard myself saying. "We'll figure out another way for you to bring in some money."

During this confusing time, I learned what it was like to walk into a supermarket and see items I wanted to buy but couldn't afford. One day, I was in Chicago, filing a brief, when I realized I might not have enough gasoline money to make it back to Normal. "I can't live this way," I whined that evening. "I'm a *lawyer*, for Christ's sake. I shouldn't have to hassle over whether it takes $2 or $3 worth of gas to get me home from court!"

Tanya glared at me. *"All my life,"* she seethed, "I've been 'hassling' over things like that. What's it *like*, Mr. Lawyer, to just say, *'fill 'er up'?"*

Driving to Chicago a week later, I was pleased to discover I had money for gas and for lunch in the bargain. "Where shall I eat?" I asked myself. "Chinese sounds good," came the answer. "If you pass a Chinese restaurant, PULL IN."

Seconds later, I spotted the New Hong Kong Buffet, a place I'd never tried. As I walked in, there seated at the table nearest the entrance was my erstwhile boss and current part-time employer, Jack Murphy.

Now I'd known and worked for Jack for several years but never shared a meal alone with him. He seemed preoccupied and rather somber. Taking some liberty, I asked him what was up. "It's a money thing," he replied.

Flashing back to my recent experiences with creditors and at the Department of Motor Vehicles, I matter-of-factly suggested Jack just come right out with his predicament to whatever employees or business associates stood to be affected. Making a great leap (which, in my spiritual oblivion, seemed like no leap at all), I told him, "If the firm was a *family,* you'd just round us all up and say, 'Uncle Jack's got a problem.'"

Jack seemed to shrug off the suggestion. But I left that restaurant no less puffed up—convinced that God had sent me there to deliver a spiritual message! That I'd just done, for Jack Murphy, what the woman at the DMV had done for me.

14

Whom Do You Love?

At one trance circle, I told Mr. Dillon I was feeling confused about life's purpose . . . more particularly, my own. I wondered what I was missing—if I was even asking the right questions.

"Do you love your wife?" Dillon responded, seeming to change the subject.

"Yes," I answered after a brief pause.

"Then what else is there to ask . . . or to know?"

The ultimate purpose of life, Dillon seemed to be saying, was to love—not in some abstract, agape sense, but in relation to another specific human being. His spiritual teaching thus differed from the Eastern philosophies I'd encountered. The latter discouraged relational entanglements, viewing them as distractions from what should be the aspirant's single-minded yearning for God.

But Dillon posited relationship as an ideal venue within which to develop our spirituality. He saw the householder's worldly responsibilities as a natural hedge against selfishness. Our very entanglements should help inoculate us against hedonism, preventing sensation from drowning out all receptivity to the needs of our significant others.

My own father sired four children and was married to the same woman for 51 years. But he never repented of his hedonism. When the issue of his drinking occasionally came up, his defense was that he didn't *have* to drink, but rather *chose* to.

Now did the fact he could say such a thing mean he didn't love us? Or was he doing the best he could? And did our willingness to continue interacting with him, long after we'd reached ages at which we had a say in the matter, mean we loved him more than he loved us? Or were we co-dependent gluttons for punishment, no less choosing relation with him than he was choosing his alcohol over us?

We'll all put up with more mistreatment from family members than from a stranger on the bus. More from our boss than our neighbor. The question always reduces to, "What have we to gain and what to lose by the continuation or termination of this relationship?"

Most of the time, these deliberations are subconscious. But one interaction with my father, shortly before we left the community, taught me to deal more forthrightly with the perennial questions, "Is this relationship redeemable? Should I risk further pain for the possibility of experiencing love with this person?"

My 1983 taxes were in arrears, and the IRS had now placed a lien on our house. I knew my dad had some money saved up. What about asking him for some help?

The likelihood of a positive response seemed remote—that of a contemptuous rebuke all but certain. But it had been a long time since I'd asked Dad for anything (other than to sober up). Suppose I were to approach him, this time, about my predicament instead of his own. With the kind of straightforwardness I'd summoned for the patrons at the Department of Motor Vehicles.

There was a big difference, of course, between that inter-action and the one now under consideration. My father and I had a history. It's probably easier to stand on the corner and beg from strangers than to confront our more personal demons by approaching "our own" for help.

But the good fairy was nudging me to take this risk—to give my dad and myself one more opportunity to grow. Her challenge went something like this:

What if God is standing by, ready to support (but not initiate) a miracle. Waiting to give your father the gentle boost he needs if you can just approach him nonjudgmentally. With the common respect he's not been shown in years, especially by a member of his own family.

Imagine the potential healing if he could then find the wherewithal to part with some of his false securi-ty. Not because he "had to"—not because you deman-ded it. Because he *chose* to. Because, in the light of your vulnerability, his own love unexpectedly surged ahead of his fear.

And think what such a turn of events would mean to you, Adam. This isn't some stranger at the DMV— this one's *your* daddy (who already *is* addicted). But that sober reality needn't deny him (or you) the op-portunity to rise to the occasion.

"Don't be a shmuck," the bad fairy cut in. "The reason beggars stand on street corners is, they know better than to bang their heads against a stone wall. You'd be smarter to join them than to call your father—you might actually raise some cash! In all events, the rejection of a passing stranger would be a lot less painful than one more kick in the teeth from *that* asshole."

The good fairy won. I made the call. My dad was sober. So far so good. I spoke to him with more emotional candor than I had since early childhood. And he listened, with uncharacteristic patience.

After a few moments' discussion, Dad said: "Here's what I want you to do. You call the IRS and arrange to pay them $300 a month for the next two years. I can't give you any of my saved-up money. But I'll send half my Social Security check, and you can use that to pay off the IRS."

That conversation was a miracle I cherish to this day. But in the mail a few days later came the following note: "I can't do it. It's *not* that I don't love you. Please understand."

I burst into tears when I read the above. But I also knew this communication was a second miracle, equal to the first. It had been a long time since my dad and I had offered our best to each other. Since we'd both found the wherewithal to acknowledge our love . . . in the very *face* of our limitations.

15

The End of the Beginning

The rabbis of the Talmud used to say, *"Im eyn kemach, eyn Torah"*– "Without bread, there can *be* no spirituality." This is a lesson our community never grasped. Instead of all going out and getting full-time jobs, we lurched from one financial crisis to another. Our still intense, still important communal processes felt increasingly like they were taking place on the deck of the Titanic.

But this was the roaring '80s, when the banks were falling all over themselves to lend money. Each time I became convinced the ship really was going down, a letter would arrive, informing me that in light of my "excellent payment history," my credit line was being increased. (And on each such occasion, I'd ask myself whether this was God, throwing me another lifeline, or Satan, luring me farther out to sea.)

Having come this far, I don't believe I'd have given up on the community based on our financial distress, standing alone. But two other issues arose that made it impossible for me to remain part of Tanya and Sherman's camp.

The first was ideological. A senior member of the group announced, with their apparent blessing, that he was leaving his wife. Her lagging spiritual progress was preventing him from realizing his own fullest potential. So he'd decided "to put God and spiritual purpose first"—even though Dillon himself had pronounced this couple "eternal soulmates."

And on that point, everything else now seemed to teeter. This wasn't the first of our couples to have gone their separate ways. But those prior partings had been bittersweet, amounting to an acknowledgment (*ipso facto*) that the relationship had run its *karmic* course. Having thus completed their growth-work together, the former spouses were now a step closer to finding their *true* (eternal) soulmates.

This was both the paradox and the genius of the eternal soulmate construct. So long as the couple stayed together, no one questioned their eternal status. But the community demanded they *act* like eternal soulmates—according to our strict behavioral and energetic standard. Which, in turn, put the couple's staying power constantly to the test. So that however long they lasted, the presumptive soulmates lived on an exhilarating marital edge.

But *this* clever man had exacted a cosmic guarantee . . . that his love for his wife *would* stand the test of time. As if being dead somehow made Dillon that smart.*

The demise of this relationship should thus have taught us (and *Dillon*) a profound lesson. Instead, it put the lie to the entire spiritual premise.

"Such inability of soulmates to progress together is extremely *rare,"* Dillon gravely declared. Then he purported to annul this aberrational relationship.

*As noted in Chapter 5, I had similarly outsmarted myself.

Such facile revisionism cast every assumption I'd made about what we were all doing together into serious doubt. If a spiritually ordained, eternal soulmate relationship could fail, even after the enlightened and intensive care we'd all given it, something was seriously amiss. How could such a contradiction be so blithely rationalized by Dillon (and accepted by Tanya and Sherman)? And if a senior member of the group could so summarily dump his own eternal soulmate, what must that say about the commitment he'd only derivatively made to me and mine?

The final straw was a confrontation between Sherman and me. As a follow-up to the couples counseling Diane and I had done at Purdue, she was asked to teach a formal course in family dynamics. This time, she invited not just me, but Tanya and Sherman to team-teach the course with her.

True to our convictions, we structured the course around the theme of honest communication. So I shouldn't have been surprised when, a month or two into the semester, one of the students took me aside and invited me to walk my talk. He asked why Diane and I seemed to defer, at every turn, to Tanya and Sherman. "They appear to be *controlling* you," the student boldly asserted.

This young man was certainly going out on a limb to share such an observation. He knew nothing of our history with Tanya and Sherman and had no apparent ax to grind. "We defer out of respect for their insight and experience," I tentatively responded.

But when I recounted the above on the way home from class, Sherman's reaction all but made the student's case.

"You betrayed me," he declared, with little affect and even less circumspection. "You should have acknowledged me, forthrightly, as your spiritual teacher. And told the student that as such, it was fine with you to be controlled by me."

We rode the rest of the way home in stunned silence. I waited a few days for the dust to settle, hoping Sherman would get in touch with just how out of control his ego had become. Instead, the standoff escalated.

The family that had been sharing our home abruptly gathered up its belongings and moved out. This without benefit of five minutes' process, though we'd endured countless hours of tortured soul-searching with them over the most trifling issues of daily life.

The man who'd quit his night job at the post office with my blessing now refused to let his little daughter *play* with our toddler son. A woman who'd been nursemaid and aunt to our infant removed her coffee maker and dishtowels from our house. And never held our baby again.

The weeks and months that followed were the bitterest of our lives. I've weighed, long and hard, my gains, losses, choices and responsibility for all I experienced in the community. Whether I could have learned what I learned there at less personal cost, I cannot say.

I know only that the above incident shattered my illusion of accountability with this group of people. And that any further growth there would not have been worth the price.

PART THREE

WORKING
WITHOUT A NET

16

Two Little Pigs

Looking back on this difficult time, I believe my greatest challenge was to separate the wheat from the chaff of the preceding three years. But our first priority was to re-establish diplomatic relations with our "blood" families—if they'd have us back. And I'd have to explain myself to Jack Murphy, in the hope I still had a full-time job to return to.

While packing up for our move back to the city, I came across some correspondence to my older brother in which I'd attempted to explain our previous relocation (to Normal):

Dear Frank,

One of the things I so admire about Murphy and Green is their open-mindedness about the lifestyle we've opted for. The day I told Murphy I wanted to go part-time, he held his calls for twenty minutes to hear the saga of our move to Normal, our relationship to the community gathered here and the circumstances that had brought me to my decision. I told him about Mr. Dillon and the influence he's had on our marriage and values. Then I steeled myself for a skeptical, if not outright disparaging response.

After hearing me out, Murphy squared himself in his seat, locking me eyeball to eyeball. "You know, Adam, if you'd told me all this shit the first day you walked into this office . . . " Jack paused to spit a mouthful of tobacco into his cup, and I clutched the sides of my chair, waiting for the other shoe to drop . . . "we'd still be sitting here having this conversation."

I appreciated Murphy's gesture and regretted not having been more candid with him at our initial meeting. Of course, I'd never lied to him about anything; I'd just talked about wanting to live in a smaller town, etc.—the same rationales we gave you for the move to Normal. It seems time, now, to let you in on the rest of the story:

*Diane and I came here (1) to work on our relationship. After twelve years, it was barely hanging by a thread. We hoped to make a fresh start, this time putting our marriage ahead of everything else; (2) to learn to **be** more authentic, first and foremost, with each other. That meant getting a handle on neurotic behaviors, the unconscious as well as the conscious, that have dominated our communication for most of our married life; (3) to enhance our self-awareness (bringing the unconscious **into** consciousness) by trusting our feelings the way we've previously trusted only thoughts and opinions. (From this perspective, the heart has more to offer than the mind, and loving trumps "telling it like it is."); (4) to share our personal and relational process with others similarly com-*

mitted, thereby creating an extended family environment for ourselves and our son; (5) to share, also, our material things, in the hope of outgrowing our selfishness; (6) to overcome petty ego, trading the illusion of gross control for a subtler, less provincial sense of purpose. In short: (7) to put more faith in God, realizing that our success only **seems** to spring from credentials, worry, manipulation and being in the right place at the right time.*

I could hear the wheels turning in your head, squeaking louder as you moved from number one to number seven (and perhaps by that one, lumping us with the Moonies or whomever). The truth, in all events, is that we believe in God. And while that in itself isn't news, we now try to glean spiritual content from the most prosaic of our experience. That is how we express and nourish our nascent faith.

Frank, I've been afraid to share such aspirations with you in the past. Part of my process here seems a weaning from whatever has so deterred me. I guess I haven't wanted to hear you accuse me of being "in need of professional help."

Which of these tenets would I still claim were I writing Frank today, from the carnage of our failed utopian experiment? And in approaching him now, would I concede that he'd been right to condemn it?

I found and re-read his letter answering the above:

---

* We came to Normal with one son but left with three.

Adam,

There's a difference between being open-minded and empty-headed. I think your current lifestyle follows the pattern you established earlier of chasing after false gods and relying on phony "support" groups for "love and guidance." Sorry, but I believe problems related to self-image/self-respect are best dealt with in a one-to-one relationship with a competent psychiatrist.

This is not an "accusation"; it's loving, caring, sound counsel. Healthy individuals don't need nor desire to "share" such intimacies as you describe with groups. People—healthy, emotionally mature people—establish appropriate boundaries.

I'm struck by the vague psychobabble that threads its way through your letter, e.g., the "illusion of control" and "the heart has more to offer than the mind." Your dogma is, of course, anti-reason precisely because it is unreasonable!

*But of your seven tenets, the last two concern me the most—because you, my brother, aren't "overcoming" ego, you're **wallowing** in it; and because healthy people don't give over their control—not to gurus, ghosts, groups or gods—not to **anyone**—not **ever**! It's when we abandon our own reason and are content to rely on external authority that trouble begins.*

I share these feelings with you because I care about you and want to see you grow up already and take charge of your own life. Bertrand Russell wrote:

"There is something feeble and a little contemptible about a man who cannot face the perils of life without the help of comfortable myths. Almost inevitably, some part of him is aware that they are myths and that he believes them only because they are comforting. But he dare not face this thought! Moreover, since he is aware, however dimly, that his opinions are not rational, he becomes furious when they are disputed."

*Adam, you are so intelligent, articulate and gifted. Get some **real** help for the emotional needs. As they say around here, "Wake up and smell the coffee!" And spare me the spiritual sloganeering—don't engage me in polemics. I can't validate your mishoogas!**

> Love,
> Your brother, Frank

As I read the above today, I see both the love and the wisdom in my brother's message (though I still chafe at his rigidity in the face of my *mishoogas*). But my response at the time was just as Bertrand Russell had predicted:

Dear Frank,

I'll try to keep my polemics to a minimum. The difference between us is that you view belief in God as unreasonable, immature and a symptom of mental illness. If there is a God, what could possibly be unhealthy about wanting to subordinate one's personal will to His? On the other hand, what's so healthy and

---

* Yiddish for nonsense (craziness).

responsible about "establishing appropriate bounda-
ries" (with everyone but the recommended psychia-
trist)?

   You sing the praises of psychiatry (which you've
not experienced) at the same time you condemn the
spirit (to which you've likewise never been exposed).
If that's not the height of presumptuousness, I'm defi-
nitely wallowing in something.

Your brother, Adam

*P.S. **Fuck** Bertrand Russell.*

As I'll relate in a later chapter, I've long since obtained
the recommended one-on-one with the competent psychiatrist. I'm fairly confident the good doctor would today give
me a decent bill of mental health. But will my brother nevertheless conclude, from all I've written here, that I'm still
to be counted among the purveyors of psychobabble? (And
what would Bertrand Russell say?)

   However our relationship may continue to unfold, in
1986, I had to call on Frank for financial help to get back
on my feet. I felt like the little pig who had built with
sticks, importuning the one who'd built with bricks. Some
part of me dimly sensed that I'd laid some solid (if half-
baked) bricks of my own. But for the present, they were affording my family and me no shelter and little comfort.

17

Practice Makes Perfect

We thus swallowed more pride and gratefully accepted help from both my brothers, my sister, my mother and Diane's parents. I went back to Murphy & Green and was relieved to find their door still open to me.

At the firm over the next few years, I kept my nose to the grindstone, reassuring my employers I still had what it took professionally. I outlasted the jibes about searching for "higher authorities" and resumed the persona of the scholarly, if eccentric legal analyst and writer. I got good results on some complex cases, published an article in the Loyola Law Journal and stood poised to reclaim my professional *bona fides*.

But some part of me, unrepentant of my past and uncertain of my worldly direction, found it difficult to confine myself to the straight and narrow of professional life. I was frustrated by the limited occasion it was affording me for interaction with other human beings.

This may come as a surprise to those whose image of lawyers derives from the O.J. Simpson trial. The fact is, even "litigators" spend most of their time sequestered at their desks, poring over documents of one sort or another.

There are scores of these hours for each one spent in lively, argumentative banter.

In addition, most lawyers tend toward emotional reticence. This is partly a function of the law's emphasis on analytical skills. It is, after all, our ability as thinkers, not as feelers, for which we're remunerated. Nevertheless, while I hardly expected the kind of self-revealing processes that had been the staple of my interactive diet in the community, I found the paucity of non-legal communication among lawyers to be the other end of the interpersonal spectrum.

The time came for me to be considered for partnership. This is, in law firm culture, what tenure is in academia. Partnership would thus place the firm's and, by extension, the legal community's imprimatur on my professional achievements. Given the slow, if scenic career path I'd taken, I craved the recognition and sense of identity that "making partner" would finally afford me.

But my dissatisfaction with the interpersonal pedestrianism of law practice (and perhaps my inability to let things go too smoothly for too long) got the better of me. It occurred to me I might be happier as a judge than I'd been as an attorney.

It also happened, just at that time, that there were an unusual number of openings on the Cook County Circuit Court. I had some political contacts in the Governor's Office, where those appointments would be made. But the current administration was also nearing the end of its term.

This put me in a kind of "catch 22." To be a viable candidate for the bench, I'd need strong support from my current employers, Jack Murphy and Jack Green. But this was hardly the time to be discussing with them my desire to be working somewhere else. If such candor were to cost me my partnership, it might dash, at the same stroke, any prospect I had for a judicial appointment.

As I ruminated on this dilemma, it struck me as the same moment (another layer of the onion) I'd faced when applying for the job at Murphy & Green in the first place. Would I share any more of myself now than I had then? Or would I be hearing Jack Murphy say, down the road, "Of course we'll support you for judge; but if you'd told us this two years ago, we'd gladly have supported you then"?

Thus determined to practice what I'd preached in the letter to my brother Frank, I concluded that making partner was of little value if it required me to stifle my legitimate conflicts and ambitions. So I requested a meeting with Jack Murphy, Jack Green and the head of the firm's litigation section, Kevin O'Reilly.

They did question my commitment to the firm in the light of my interest in the bench. But the discussion was fair, frank and healthy. Afterwards, I tried to capture the essence of our conversation in the following:

MEMORANDUM

TO:	*JLM, JJG and KMO*
FROM:	*AP*
DATE:	*June 16, 1989*
RE:	*Partnership and Commitment*

Some further thoughts on the "commitment" my nomination for partnership now puts at issue. For me, this isn't just about the financial responsibility/opportunity that a partnership implies. We've done a pretty decent job, so far, keeping food on our respective tables. Having tested each other to that extent, the partnership question, it seems to me, now ups the ante for all of us—precisely by moving the discussion beyond the breadwinning per se.

So when Jack M. says he needs partners "who will be there to share the load with him," I frankly think there's a deeper statement he's trying to make. Isn't a partnership about working for each other's success as an end in itself (obviously while pursuing our own success)?

*What I'm saying is that "financial commitment" is an oxymoron. We've all got financial obligations, but commitment is something personal. Those who are with you for economic advantage, however mutual, will be gone the moment their self-interest so dictates. So if you ever **are** left holding the bag, it will be because you surrounded yourselves with people who were obligated but **not** personally committed.*

This isn't just semantics. Loyalty is a function of relationship in a way that promises, agreements, even performance can never be. Maybe that's why convincing you I'm the productive equal of this person or that has been the most unpleasant part of "making partner." Such internal competitiveness may get you a collection of brilliant lawyers, trial lawyers, rain-

makers and worker bees, but it doesn't engender loy-alty. For once the rainmaker convinces you (and him-self) that he **is** *a rainmaker, why should he stay and make rain* **with you***?*

Jack G. was right: The discussion was less about my desire to be a judge than my need to say these things to you three. Relationship and prosperity aren't mutually exclusive, and I've got no bone to pick with financial security as a goal. As Jack M. apt-ly put it, we wouldn't be beating our brains out toge-ther if we were all rich (instead of argumentative).

But just as you need partners who will be there for the bottom line, I need partners whose success cannot but grow with mine. What that means in this context is still muddled for me, but perhaps the above will give it a backdrop for some further clarification.

I probably expended thirty non-billable hours on this ef-fort to articulate, in the seemingly unreceptive environment of a busy law practice, ideals that had become part of me in the community. Kevin O'Reilly, who was valedictorian of his law school class, claimed not to understand a word of my memo. Nevertheless, he canceled a trip out of town to be there for the partners' meeting at which I'd be voted in or out . . . and spearheaded the effort in my behalf.

I did also apply for the bench. But the commission that vets judicial candidates for the Governor couldn't get past my recent stint as a spiritual communist.

My interview seemed to go smoother the second time I applied—the community never even came up. "Yeah," Jack Murphy quipped when I still didn't make the cut. "They must have powwowed before you got there: 'Here comes the *nut* case . . . let's not rile him!'"

18

Process and Prosperity

My partnership memo and related conversations weren't the first time I'd presumed to smuggle interpersonal process into the professional workings of Murphy & Green. When I first joined the firm, in 1983, three other recruits had come aboard at the same time. So Jack and Jack had left it to us to determine the order in which our names would appear on the letterhead.

Our foursome consisted of two recent graduates (one of whom had previously clerked for the firm), a lawyer who'd practiced several years in another state and me, with more gray hair than all the others combined. Someone proposed we draw straws and be done with this uncomfortable business. I suggested we first take a few minutes, over lunch, to find out whether any of our names *should* come ahead of the others on the letterhead.

The woman who had clerked for the firm thought such tenure might entitle her to seniority for letterhead purposes. But the other recent grad had clerked for one of Chicago's larger, more prominent firms. When his peers there had questioned his decision to go with the young upstarts, Murphy & Green, he'd assured them that in just a few years, they'd see his name near the top of the much shorter M & G letterhead.

"Leapfrogging the three of you would get me off to a fabulous start!" he enthused. Then, more pensively, he added, "and it would impress the *hell* out of my old man."

The lawyer who'd practiced in another state was also surprisingly candid. He didn't much care where his name turned up on the letterhead. His only concern was that so passive a stance, were it to leave the room, might raise questions about his adversarial zeal!

Seeing the merit in each of my colleagues' positions, I suggested my name come last . . . and that they continue discussing the proper order for theirs. Pandemonium ensued. You'd have thought I'd pulled a revolver and pointed it at my temple! It became a matter of utmost urgency for them to talk me out of my position—lest they be perceived as having taken unfair *advantage* of me.

In the face of this uproar (and realizing the lunch hour was almost over), I volunteered to break the logjam by going *first* on the letterhead. We all had a good laugh, then proceeded to draw straws.

The meeting thus concluded with the same result (and yet a totally different feeling) than if we'd just drawn straws in the first place. I don't remember the order in which our names ended up. Fifteen years later, I'm the only one of the four still on the letterhead (which today, in all events, is alphabetical). But I do know no one left that meeting feeling short-changed by the outcome.

Looking back on these, my prime breadwinning years, it occurs to me that "climbing the letterhead" has meant no more (and no less) than squaring my lofty pronouncements with my own productivity on a sustainable basis. When all is said and done, that's what walking one's talk means in the business and professional world.

And what of those whose economic fate was riding on my ability to reconcile what I'd learned in the community with my professional and worldly obligations? Before embarking on an interactive course that threatened to impact them financially, I'd convene a family meeting. The agenda was to ascertain whether they were *with* me in the proposed course of action. I'd lay out all the risks, like the hospital does when you go in for surgery. I'd ask each son what he thought I should do—and whether he was willing to absorb his share of the economic blow if things turned out badly.

In that way, the memo to Jack, Jack and Kevin was not from me alone, but from me, Diane and my boys.

19

Worrying Wisely

"Worry is the worst murderer of mankind," Mr. Dillon used to declare. Pop-psychology and New-Age culture likewise tend to demonize stress, implying that the more we worry, the sicker we become (until eventually we *die* of something). But Dillon was also fond of reminding us that "there *is* no death and there are no dead." In that case, what's the harm of a little worry now and then—especially if it gets us in gear to accomplish something in our physical interim?

Over the years at Murphy & Green, I've conducted an orientation session for our new lawyers. The challenge is to give the fresh troops a realistic sense of the focus and productivity a successful practice demands, without driving them further into the survival mentality that's already got them scared half to death. But one point I feel obliged to get across is that a due quotient of worry accompanies every file in our office. The discussion goes something like this:

> You may think the people at the top of the hierarchy have all the worries, but it's really the other way around. If there's a file I've not found time to get to,

my worry meter starts buzzing every time I glance in its direction. But the second I hand that file off to you, the worry, like so much toxic radon emanating from the earth below, migrates from my office *into yours*.

Now you'll be getting assignments from a number of partners, none of whom will be losing much sleep over how you're reconciling their competing demands on your time. It'll be your responsibility to deal with both the sensational and the relational implications of the resultant stress.

In other words, you must *feel* (stay conscious of) the pressure. In large measure, it's what keeps us on top of what we're being paid to stay on top of. But you've also got to remain conscious of your own needs and limitations. That means monitoring the impact, both here and in your larger context, of all we're demanding of you.

This too is part of good lawyering. And it can be a fine line between impressing us with your uncomplaining industry and having the good sense to say, "I just can't *do* all that you're asking of me."

I then wistfully tell them about a time Jack Murphy had asked how *I* was coming on a particular project. I'd responded, matter-of-factly, that I still had two other assignments ahead of his. As I turned to walk away, Jack stopped me. "Uh, Adam," he asked haltingly, "who's *worrying* about that file—you or me?"

"I'll tell you what," I shot back. "It's going to take me a week and a half to get to that file. If you want me to worry about it in the meantime, I can do that. But it's also fine with me if *you* want to do the worrying."

Caught off guard by my *chutzpah*, Jack gave a confused shrug and walked away.

Now few other associates would have risked such impudence with the senior partner of the firm. But this was during my community days, when I was buoyed by a false sense of security. When the shit eventually hit the fan, I had to come to grips, once again, with the dilemma facing every other mortal being: Which files are mine, which are Jack Murphy's and which are *God's?* How *much* worrying should I be doing, about what . . . and in what order?

I thus found myself relating differently to Murphy when he summoned me, not too many years later, for a meeting with an important client. The firm was then housed in two separate buildings, about a block apart. So I started jogging, briefcase in tow, from my building over to Jack's.

Struck by my own unseemly sense of urgency, I remarked to myself, "You're a 'grown attorney'—why so nervous about a meeting with 'the boss' and his 'important client'?"

Except that I was out of breath, the meeting was routine, resulting in the transfer to me of a box of documents relevant to a potential lawsuit. I set the box on the rear seat of my car, intending to peruse the material at home, over the weekend.

A day or so later, I got a frantic call from Diane. "Something terrible has happened," she began. "I was driving on the parkway, and the door of the car just *flew open!"*

Picturing one of my kids flying out, it was a relief to learn that the box of documents was the only casualty. "Your papers," Diane somberly reported, "are all over the Expressway."

Now these were original files, reflecting a ten-year history of transactions between the parties to the prospective litigation. They were irreplaceable. I couldn't imagine how I was going to break this news to Jack Murphy, especially after the fuss he (and I) had seemed to be making to impress this particular client.

With no pressing deadline in the case, I thought I'd wait for some inspiration (or lightning) to strike me. I didn't have to wait long. Within a day or so, Jack called to say the client was back, with some further thoughts he wanted to share with us about the case. This time, it was a long, slow walk over to Jack's office.

"You owe me a hundred bucks," Jack said as I entered the room.

"A hundred bucks?" I restated. "Did we have a bet about something?"

"No," Jack drawled, "a hundred bucks is what I just handed Richard, here. He gave his own $100 to some *fireman* . . . who showed up at his **house** this morning . . . WITH THAT BOX OF DOCUMENTS WE GAVE **YOU** THE OTHER DAY!"

Years later, at a firm retreat, Jack and I were reminiscing about this incident. I reminded him how he'd summoned me to that initial client meeting—like some smart nerd he kept on the payroll for just such occasions.

"If you need to show off for your clients like that, I'm willing to play the part for you from time to time," I assured him. "I just can't predict what outside forces may intervene to sabotage both our expectations!"

"And what *you* need to know," Jack responded affectionately, "is that I'm willing to do the same for you whenever you need me to." That's when I knew I really had "made partner."

Jack gave me one other gift that night. He thanked me for a conversation we'd had years earlier. "You know the one I mean—over lunch that day . . . in the *Chinese restaurant.*"

20

Pills and Process

Some time in the early '90s, my brother Earl went through an emotional crisis. I heard myself advising him, as our elder brother had counseled me, to see a psychiatrist. In thus recommending the very one-on-one, professional relationship I'd rejected for myself, I was reminded of a story I'd heard at *satsang*.

A woman was at wit's end with her young son, who only wanted to eat sweets. Her guru suggested she bring the boy to him, but not for two weeks. At the appointed time, the child was so moved by the guru's words, he promptly cut his candy intake by half.

Years later, the woman reminded the guru of the impact he'd had on her now grown (and healthy) son. "I've always wondered though, Master, why you made me wait the two weeks before bringing him to see you."

"When you first mentioned your boy to me," the guru answered, "my own sweet tooth was out of control. I needed time to clean up *my* eating habits before I could speak to your son about his!"

It was thus my younger brother's distress, rather than my elder's cajoling, that led me, gently but firmly, to my decision. I simply couldn't help but notice how similar my own eating habits were to Earl's.

It seems almost comical, looking back, that after a guru, a ghost and all the accompanying *mishoogas,* it took a simple look in the mirror of my younger brother's eyes to recognize and accept my clinical predicament . . . and begin clicking the heels of my own ruby slippers.

I walk a fine line in so describing my decision to "get help" of this more mainstream sort. I've not arrived at Chapter 20 to recant the psychospiritual convictions I've gone to such lengths to relate. The fact is, I don't see a contradiction between them and the more conventional course I was now set upon.

Had I established the "appropriate one-to-one relationship" twenty years earlier, I might be a different person today, but not necessarily a better, happier or wiser one. (And what kind of movie would it have been had Dorothy clicked her heels three times before ever meeting the Tin Man or dealing with the Wicked Witch of the West?)

I had met Dr. Blumenthal some years before. In the aftermath of our break with Tanya and Sherman, I'd reported to the Jewish Family Service for an assessment of my psychological condition. After a few visits with a social worker, Blumenthal was called in for a consultation.

But I'd come to that session directly from a deposition. After observing thirty seconds of my upbeat, adrenaline-boosted demeanor, he pronounced me "not-depressed"; and left the social worker and me to our own further devices.

I didn't hold that against him when I was finally ready to get into ongoing treatment. So for the next few years, we took a more in-depth look at those parallel personas (spiritual and worldly) that I'd first discussed with Sarah. And my inability to find satisfaction, for very long, on either track.

I came to understand that my spiritual leanings were symbolically but perniciously linked to my mother, the nurturer. My ambitious side was staunchly associated with my father, the provider. But his providence came at a Faustian price. Nightly, he'd rave that the greenback was God (and peace of mind, the *rich* man's booty). Setting no store in his affection, I'd vowed to earn some scant respect. Someday, somehow, I would "show him the money."

Mother, not surprisingly, was Father's better half. Like TV's Mr. Rogers, she loved us just the way we were. "Life is what you make it," she chirped, "so do what makes you *happy.*"

She was there for us at school events our father never came to. Still, I heard his muffled groan beneath the weight of her good cheer.

But then, as I moved from adolescence into adulthood, Mother's focus took an inexplicable turn. She stopped inquiring about my vocal or religious pursuits and now began each conversation by asking how things were going for me *at work.* For some reason, this always felt like a punch in the stomach.

Blumenthal helped me see that I experienced such inquiries as a betrayal of the spiritual alliance I thought Mother and I had forged. Her values were actually much closer to Dad's than I'd ever imagined. And it was a slippery slope from there to an even more devastating realization: that the two were no less aligned in his nightly atrocities.

So long as my psyche had Mother pegged as "good" and Dad as "bad," I was as stuck as they were in their relational homeostasis. I'd have to keep the values and aspirations associated with each parent at cross-purposes—just as Gerald and Abby had always seemed to be. I thus lived in a state of chronic ambivalence, siding mostly with Mother's more "spiritual" paradigm, but with an undermining cache of loyalty to Dad's more cynical worldview.

Important as the above insights were for me, my "quality of life" was impacted less by them than by Prozac. This time, Blumenthal prescribed it for me at the very start of treatment. But it was only after some twelve weeks that I experienced a remarkable and rather sudden shift in my emotional sensation. I use that phrase to convey that the improvement seemed to have nothing to do with my relationships *per se,* or how I was conducting them.

Simply put, I felt well. Not the exhilaration that accompanied a victory in court. Nor the "blissed-out" state at the feet of the guru. This was an unvarnished sense of well-being, unrelated to any notion of earning *or* grace. It was like coming into some emotional nest egg—one that had been accruing interest all those years it had gone unclaimed.

The transformation was all the more astonishing for the fact that in the three full months it took the Prozac to kick in, I hadn't been in any acute distress. It was as if someone had just flipped a switch . . . and every positive thing in my life was suddenly shouting, "SURPRISE!"

My ardent inner process seemed abruptly obsolete. Yet in my daily interactions, my energy was uncharacteristically robust. I was fully engaged. *Unconflicted.*

"What are you *on?*" Sarah asked, in a mildly accusatory tone. I'd just entered the foyer of her house, not having seen her for over a year. I didn't tell her right away it was Prozac she was sensing in my aura (though I'd brought the bottle of pills along with me).

Indeed, I'd scheduled this appointment precisely to get Sarah's take on how this medication was affecting me. I certainly knew I was feeling better but still wanted her unique kind of second opinion.

Sarah, I should mention, is an organic health nut. Her favorite goody is a glass of fresh-squeezed carrot juice. She avoids not just medications, but microwave ovens.

Nevertheless, after tuning in to these pills in my system, she conceded they were doing me some good. She added, somewhat grudgingly, that I wouldn't always need this medication.

I have my own misgivings about relying on a chemical to feel well. But there are sequelae of my emotional karma that haven't yielded to God's more spontaneous healing process. I'll continue to claim that healing with the fullest interpersonal and introspective conscientiousness of which I'm capable. No less so when I say, "Praise the Lord and pass the Prozac!"

21

Insight vs. Healing

There was one aspect of my depression that seemed to stand apart from the more endogenous illness. As the extended family assembled each year for Thanksgiving, I'd sink into a lethargic state that would last all weekend. In particular, my mother's presence seemed to bring on a distinct emotional fog.

In the spring of 1989, I was greeting relatives who had flown in for my first son's Bar Mitzvah. Spotting my mother down a long airport concourse, the degree and suddenness of my energy shift was startling. Instantly, I dropped from a state of anticipation and high intensity to one of lethargy and depression.

When I mentioned this episode to Sarah, her only insight was that it had to do with something that had occurred between Mother and me when I was 10 or 11 years old.

Out of the blue some years later, Mother invited me to unburden myself of any criticism I might have of her parenting. This was shortly after my father had died, and I suspect it had to do with some grief counseling she was getting. Mother mentioned that she was making the same communicative overture to each of her four children.

133

We were sitting out in the front yard, under an elm tree, when she thus propositioned me. Ironically, I'd been keeping our interactions to a minimum that visit—trying to ward off the kind of tailspin described above. Now, Mother was asking me not just to stop the warding off but to immerse myself in the very energy that stood between us.

An incident sprang to mind—I believe the one to which Sarah had previously alluded. Around the time of my own Bar Mitzvah (age 13, not 10 or 11), Mother had left the house after a heavier than usual course of verbal battering. But instead of drifting off into his usual, sleepy stupor, Dad went straight to the phone. I heard him say, "Hello, June? This is *Bob Schaeffer*. I'd like to see you tonight." Then he took a shower, got dressed to kill and left the house for the rest of the evening.

For the next few days, I was caught up in a crisis of conscience and divided loyalty. Should I rat out my father to my mother? Since she seemed the innocent victim of both his nightly abuse and this singular betrayal, I decided she deserved my allegiance.

Without batting an eye, Mother told me I was *mistaken* in what I'd heard. She even managed a sly chuckle over my "misinterpretation." Her friend *Joan,* who was training to be a manicurist, had been doing Dad's *nails,* for practice. Undoubtedly, it was Joan (not "June") Dad had called for this spur of the moment appointment. As for "Bob Schaeffer," that was just a stage name Dad used to go by (when Mother and Joan first met him, at the Chicago Playhouse).

That night, I heard my mother and father yelling at each other from behind their bedroom door. Only now do I realize how different, how much *healthier* this shouting match was from the nightly bombardments to which I'd long inured myself. How much more overt . . . and to the point.

At the time, though, I felt guilty—that I'd precipitated a worsening of my parents' status quo (disruption of their relational homeostasis as I'd now call it). My father was especially distant toward me in the aftermath of the first real fight he'd had with my mother in years.

Some days later, I was riding in the car with my parents. My instinct, even then, was to take initiative in the face of their communicative default. So from my position in the back seat, I searched for a way to break the ice with my father.

At age 13, I didn't know how to say, "Mom and Dad, I feel as though I'm being blamed for the problem you two are having. And I'm upset that you've left me completely in the dark about this whole awful situation." So I just said, "Dad, tell me about your days at the Chicago Playhouse!"

"DON'T TALK ABOUT THAT!" Dad shouted. For the rest of the ride, not another word was spoken. For the next *28 years,* nothing further would be said.

As I now pondered my mother's unexpected invitation to address any emotional grievance I might have, the memory of these events flooded my consciousness. After reminding her of the incident, I took a deep breath and said:

> Mother, do you see how you left me out on a limb after I'd allied myself with you in this drama? We might have taken some comfort in our shared (if quite different) aggrievement. Instead, you lied to me. Then you gave me up to the enemy.

And even after you and Dad had fought it out, you never came back to clean things up on my end. Or to reassure me that the two of you were trying to turn things around.

This was no diatribe against my mother. My words were soft and tearful. She also cried. And after only a bit of defending, took responsibility for what had transpired between us so many years before.

From that day forward, I've never suffered another depressive meltdown on coming into my mother's physical presence. That specific energy was dissipated by our belated but heartfelt communication.

I assume my remaining, more endogenous depression no less has its antecedents in specific (if cumulative) interpersonal experiences. Or in current relational circumstances the full implications of which I've not yet been ready to address. Just as medical research sifts for clues within a cancer cluster, so it behooves us to monitor our emotional fluctuations; to search out the linkage between our interactions and their psychosomatic effects. That is largely what psychotherapy attempts to do.

The healing with my mother also reminded me that identifying our emotional wounds and resolving them are two different things. Sarah had helped me connect the Bob Schaeffer incident with my ensuing emotional allergy to Mother. But just the awareness of cause and effect had afforded me no relief from the symptomatology.

In this sense, the thought and feeling are like twins separated at birth, each sensing their incompleteness. True objectivity, the kind that presages our emotional healing, entails both seeing and feeling interpersonal reality at the self-same instant.

This experience with my mother also taught me that as long as I breathe air (and so long as those with whom I may yet effect some relational healing continue, themselves, to breathe), I must take my opportunities to resolve things with those who have hurt me . . . and with those whom I have hurt.

I was attempting to do that with my parents when I asked my dad to talk to me about "Bob Schaeffer." It just took another 28 years for me to come up with a more artful approach. And for my mother, at least, to be willing to make herself vulnerable.

22

A Matter of Apples and Eggs

But how do we heal relationships with people who have died? Or who simply aren't open to process, however gentle and well meaning?

My father now fell into both categories. He'd certainly never invited any feedback about his parenting. In fact, on the one occasion I'd attempted such a communication, he called me "holier than thou." And left me with the parting benediction, *"An apple never falls far from the tree."*

I was contemplating that conversation some years later, on my ride in to work. I'd vowed that *this* little apple would move as far from the tree (and as fast) as it could thrust itself. "But how exactly *does* an apple 'thrust' itself?" I pondered, while negotiating the morning rush hour.

I had recently read *The Road Less Traveled,* by M. Scott Peck, and for no particular reason, it occurred to me that my answer had something to do with *Peck* . . . that if I'd poke around a little with this hint, the solution would be self-evident.

This kind of internal chitchat had become a habit for me by now—a harbinger of insight, urging me to stay with my subject matter, but in a relaxed sort of mental soft-focus. So I meditated on the unlikely mantra I'd been given: "Poke, poke; Peck, Peck; poke, poke; Peck, Peck . . ." until the light came on:

YOU'RE NOT AN APPLE, YOU'RE A CHICK-EN. No, wait . . . an *unborn chick* . . . growing ever more confined in its own neurotic egg! From *inside* that egg, you can "thrust" with all your might, this way and that, but like the fallen apple, you'll never roll far from where you began.

Yet if, instead of thrusting, the chick just does what comes naturally—*pokes* and *pecks* against the shell of that egg—it will, in due course, hatch. And on that day (*bayom hahu*), discover things the apple can never know . . . like *feet* (not to mention wings)!

I was so enamored of this "breakthrough," I called Diane just as soon as I got to the office. "You're not going to *believe* what I'm staring at," she said, after hearing my story. Diane had been browsing through *Newsweek* when I called, and she'd flipped—just as the phone started ringing—to this full-page illustration:

This portrait of me was part of an ad for an airline. It now sits on my desk, as a reminder.

PART FOUR

INTEGRATION

23

"Community"

The Road Less Traveled was one of those rare gifts that have inspired millions of people. I went on to read *The Different Drum; Community Making and Peace*. There, Peck attempts to distill the psychological and communicative elements that have allowed encounter groups to reach a collective psychosensory state he calls "community." When a speaking tour brought him to Chicago, I got to talk with Peck about this.

I asked him whether positing community as a process-induced, group sensation didn't reduce it to a peak experience, as opposed to something that might be sustained and integrated into normal life. He invited me to follow up with him on the issue, and in a subsequent letter, I confessed I'd had my fill of such collective peak moments.

"Of what value are these weekend workshops," I challenged, "if none of us is willing or capable of achieving what you call 'community' in our ongoing contexts? And should we not be suspicious when our communicative zeal expresses itself not in the personal conundra of everyday life, but in contrived encounters with people we don't know (and with whom we have no future)?"

Peck wrote back, inviting me to a workshop sponsored by his organization, the Foundation for Community Encouragement (FCE). So much for having had my fill of collective peak moments. I soon found myself seated in a circle of about 25 people, in Knoxville, Tennessee.

From *The Different Drum,* I had a rough idea what was in store. In the first stage of community-building, the participants display the kind of sociable, performance behavior I've described in Chapter 11. (Everyone acts as if they're already *in* the desired community state.) Peck calls this "pseudocommunity."

In stage two ("chaos"), the phoniness begins to break down. Somebody becomes impatient or otherwise confrontational, and things turn ugly.

By stage three, the participants start owning up to the fact that they've no idea what "community" is, much less how to snap themselves into it. Peck calls this "emptying." Someone finds the courage to test the waters of personal vulnerability, to communicate without pretense or manipulative agenda. And this, like a drop of water on a parched plant, somehow allows everyone else in the group to lower their own defenses.

The final stage, "community," is that rare affinity, or heightened group-sensitivity, that allows people to stop performing for and judging one another. It's a collective state in which each person's unique presence (rather than his ideas or personality) is truly felt and unconditionally accepted.

Thus informed of the community-building sequence, I came to the FCE weekend determined not to play the stage-two provocateur. But I was unable to restrain myself when a woman named Sherry, a veteran of previous FCE events, began describing the lengths to which she'd gone, over her husband's protests, to get to this workshop. Confessing her need now to obtain the community fix she'd purchased at so dear a price, she implored us to get on with the process —to move beyond the insincere banter of pseudocommunity in which we were mired. "We have only three more hours," Sherry admonished, "to *make* it . . . into *real* community."

"I DON'T GIVE A SHIT IF WE EVER GET TO SO-CALLED 'COMMUNITY'!" I heard myself erupting. "If you haven't achieved it in all the time you've had with your own husband, what good is this fleeting and artificial state you want us to induce at his further expense?"

So much for pseudocommunity. Sherry came back at me with both barrels blazing. "YOU SON OF A BITCH!" she screamed. *"WHO THE HELL DO YOU THINK YOU ARE?"*

She continued to rail against me for several minutes, without let up. But I felt no need to defend myself. My experience in Tanya and Sherman's community informed me irrefutably that this diatribe belonged not to me, but to Sherry's husband.

To be sure, my own issues had overridden my intention not to play the instigator at this event. But I'd played it in a conscious, if emotionally charged way. In point of fact, I'd accelerated the process just as Sherry had requested (confirming the old adage, "Be careful what you ask for . . . you just might *get* it!").

And our conflagration did seem to work some catharsis for the entire group. For just as soon as Sherry's outrage had dissipated, we were quite finished with the "chaos" phase and moved directly into "emptying."

The doorway was gently opened by Jan, who began describing her own marital dilemma. She was an FCE leader/ facilitator (though not officiating at this event), whose husband was chronically depressed. Jan feared he was slipping away from her; and that they wouldn't survive much longer as a couple.

Unlike the thrust and parry between Sherry and me, Jan's statement was personal and straightforward. She was neither judging her husband nor masking her own distress. Nor was she looking to the group to solve her problem or, for that matter, even to respond. Indeed, it was the very unconditionality of Jan's sharing that was about to spark us into community.

One of the group's two leaders now asked permission to step out of his role as facilitator to address an issue of his own. Apropos of my point to Sherry (and earlier, to Peck), he described his frustration at being unable to *sustain* community—not just in his everyday life, but even at these FCE events. He felt he was falling short of his calling, failing himself and those he was supposed to be serving.

This confession triggered a profuse response from an unlikely source. There was a salesman in the group, whose earlier pitch for "team spirit" (when we were stuck in pseudocommunity) had fallen rather flat. ("Our group needs a *name*," he'd gushed; "like . . . 'the Peaches'. . . or 'the *Magnolias!*'")

But the salesman's new proffer was poignant and deft. He described his own routine, driving from town to town, persuading strangers to buy things they didn't want. He was starved for some honest to God communication. And so very grateful for the last fifteen minutes of it.

At this, the facilitator burst into tears. But the salesman kept right on facilitating: "However short you may have fallen, you've done *me* a great service. I never knew straight talk like this was even possible."

The facilitator now began to wail in accompaniment. A duet, not an accompaniment—two souls, expressing their common anguish; experiencing the human dilemma, perhaps from different vantage points, but feeling it, *sharing* it. And allowing us all to share it, first through their eyes, then through our own.

As I drove to the airport for the flight home, I had a sensation of openness, from my throat to my navel. It felt as though my very guts were hanging out. For days after the event, I found it difficult to focus on the mundane activities of daily life.

We'd been warned of such a reentry phenomenon, so I was more patient with myself than I might otherwise have been. In an effort to interpret my personal state, I put pen to paper, as follows:

1. "Building community," as Peck calls it, means opening up our respective heart chakras. That chakra responds sympathetically when another's heart stirs in close proximity. If the opening is permitted to continue, the group process accelerates, as our own sympathetic vibration now sets off someone else's vibratory network.

2.   The risk of this opening is that it exposes us to pain we've been preferring not to feel. As the pupil of the eye constricts to protect us from too much or too sudden an onslaught of light, so the heart chakra constricts in the face of our emotional pain. That's the gist of our defense mechanisms. (Only in this case, it's the "darkness" that constricts and the "light" that dilates.)

3.   Nevertheless, as a pupil fixed in the wide open position would more likely blind us than enhance our vision, so the heart chakra must accommodate to ever changing interpersonal conditions. The task is to attune ourselves, ever more finely, to the amount and quality of the available light. And that is what we should mean when we speak of "setting appropriate boundaries."

24

Mutual Therapy

If the above attempts to explain the sensational experience, what (if anything) had we done together in Knoxville *relationally?* To begin with, Sherry and I wouldn't have taken each other's bait had we not each touched a sensitive nerve within the other's emotional network. I'll go so far as to suggest that Jan's subsequent sharing about her marital distress was closer to what was really on our minds, had we been prepared to address it. Instead, the two of us projected our marital issues onto each other and the group.

"Projection" is the tendency to overreact when someone else's situation or behavior threatens to remind us of our own unresolved conflict. It seems we can't help but notice in others the faults or problems we've been avoiding in our own lives.

Now if Peck is right, this isn't necessarily a bad thing, at least in the group-process setting he calls "community-building." It was the very force of Sherry's and my own projection (the "chaos" phase) that seemed to clear the way for Jan to share her marital dilemma more forthrightly. And the fact that I was personally caught up in the exchange (what the therapist would call "countertransference") didn't make my gauntlet to Sherry less timely or on point.

149

As discussed in Chapter 11, reacting emotionally to the patient's process is something the therapist is trained to guard against. But this very self-monitoring may also help guide him to the real issues. For by noticing when his own buttons are being pushed, the therapist actually *intuits* what is going on with the patient.

Now if, as Dr. Peck suggests in *The Road Less Traveled,* "any genuinely loving relationship is one of mutual psychotherapy," the management of countertransference is something we must all come to grips with. For it's inevitable, indeed desirable, that we become emotionally engaged in our loved-one's process. A process in which we, unlike the therapist, have both a personal and a lifelong stake.

But "mutual therapy" is further complicated by the fact that the communication is a two-way street. Unlike the therapist, we're called not just to monitor our emotions but to voice them. And it's that very give-and-take that tends to bring us to the therapist (or the marriage counselor) in the first place. In short, it's much harder to *have* a relationship than to counsel one.

That said, objectivity and emotionality needn't be at cross-purposes, much less mutually exclusive. What the conventional wisdom overlooks is that maintaining objectivity, once the emotional dust has been kicked up, is a spiritual, not a psychological challenge. It's about keeping the ego, not the emotions, in check.

Ego is the mother of all defense mechanisms. When a conflict erupts, it circles like a vulture, hoping to subvert the parties' will to communicate. And when it penetrates our emotional field, defensiveness is the behavioral product. Defensiveness is our neurotic stasis energized by projection, then commandeered by ego. It is emotion gone bad.

Our very reactivity to someone else's communication thus alerts us that objectivity is, to that extent, *at risk*. But the interaction may yet prove a blessing, depending on what happens next. If we hand ego the reins, our relational work-in-process degenerates into defensiveness, sabotaging the communication. But if ego can be contained, emotion will *ripen* . . . into the same intuition on which the therapist ultimately relies.

In this sense, all emotion is nascent intuition. Intuition, in turn, is emotion, inuring itself to ego so as to attain its wisdom. And such wisdom—born of emotion, not intellect—lights the way to our eventual healing.

25

Addiction

I got a nice card from Sherry a week or so after the FCE workshop. She and her husband were leaving for three days at a cabin on their favorite lake. "Now I know we have that time to reach community together," she wrote.

My own catharsis from the Knoxville encounter had less to do with my marriage than with an issue Blumenthal and I had been exploring. He'd pointed out an addictive quality to my pursuit of intensity in relationships—how I seemed to use interpersonal process to gain some temporary relief from my depression. I thus found myself wondering, both during the weekend and afterwards, whether I'd just fallen off the wagon. (This was the primary conflict I'd projected onto Sherry, the moment she displayed her own addictive craving for community.)

One of the most eloquent speakers at the Knoxville FCE event was Keith Miller, author of *The Taste of New Wine* and other Christian spiritual books. Miller's very topic was addiction, and he noted that one could be addicted to intensity, as well as to alcohol, drugs, food, sex or other sensations. He defined addiction as "any behavior that makes you feel better but isn't in your best interest . . . and which you cannot seem to stop."

Was I, then, the one palming process off as intimacy? The thought of so perverting my hard won insight was sobering indeed. I searched for a way to temper the addictive component of my own communicative zeal.

The answer I came up with was to monitor not the intensity of my interactions, but my motivation going into them. Was my agenda relational or sensational? (Did it involve a "who" or merely a "what"?)

If it was sensation I was after, then I was using people— merely pretending to relate. But if my goal was truly to communicate (taking account of the other person's needs and interests, not just my own), I needn't abstain from the ensuing interpersonal commotion.

And of course, the subtlety with which ego insinuates itself into even our most well-meaning interactions would have ruled out total abstinence in all events.

26

Feelers and Thinkers

In the early, happy days of Tanya and Sherman's community, Mr. Dillon had a way of evening things up, so that whoever seemed to have come out on the short end of the processing stick would be given their due. This was accomplished by posing the question, "Whose gift was greater, Jesus' or Judas'?"

What Dillon meant by this was that without Judas to betray him, Jesus could not have fulfilled his purpose. Thus, when a consensus was reached as to who had played the "Jesus" and who the "Judas" of a particular transaction, the latter (assuming his energy had shifted) would be welcomed back into the fold like the prodigal son. Our pledge not to stigmatize each other was the ethical corollary of Tanya's assurance, during our first visit to the community, that "once the energy is resolved, it's as though the conflict never existed."

But we often fell short of that high moral mark, and I tended to serve, on such occasions, as the Pharisaic scapegoat. The collective judgment would be that I'd mortgaged my faith to some well-reasoned doubt; my love, to pride-driven propriety.

155

Many spiritual people tend in this way to play the "heart" off against the "mind." Faith and love are credited to the former, while the latter gets the rap for worry, doubt and having to keep our agreements. When Gurudeva Ji once had the misfortune of being sued, he commented that the law was "pure mind" (a most disheartening pronouncement for us few lawyer-devotees).

Dillon also occasionally bad-mouthed the mind, and I bought into this when I preached to my brother Frank that "the heart has more to offer." If I were writing that letter today, I'd say heart and mind no more vie with each other than do liver and kidney.

We had a version of this false dichotomy operating within our own nuclear family. When the kids were small, we played a game in which I'd try to steal their "spins." The closest translation for this would be their "smells"; but what I was after was the warm, fuzzy sensation of rubbing my face right up against theirs—preferably, just as they were awakening from a long night of "spinning."

But when our middle boy was about four, he started spurning me during these snuggling sessions, in favor of his mother. "What's so special about her?" I asked in a stern but kidding tone. "She has love spins," came the reply. "Well, what kind of spins do I have?" I demanded. "Strong spins," came the answer.

———   ———   ———   ———

If the FCE workshop in Tennessee was about husbands and wives, the one in Denver, two years later, was about parents and children. There was Alfred, a therapist, whose father had been in the SS during World War II. No chip off the old block, Alfred was soft-spoken and conciliatory. Then there was Gene, who was bitter about his mother's parenting. "Her best just wasn't good enough," was Gene's angry mantra.

True to form, I again played the antagonist. For about half an hour, Alfred had been moderating our pseudocommunity, as if to fill a perceived leadership vacuum. When I finally called him on this, I sounded much more like his father, the Nazi, than I'd intended. The group leapt to Alfred's defense, declaring that he was coming "from his heart"; whereas I was obviously quite stuck "in my mind."

Henry, a retired rabbi with some standing in FCE circles, eventually spoke up for me. Remembering me from the Tennessee event, he served as a kind of character reference.

Henry admitted that on first making my acquaintance, he too had felt threatened by my penchant for cutting to the interactive chase. Nevertheless, he now suggested it was the group that was stuck, in a picture of what "heart" was supposed to look like: permissive, not percussive; comforting, not confrontational.

Temperamentally, Henry is more the conciliator than the antagonist, making him *Alfred's* more natural ally in this debate. Indeed, his defection to my side of the heart-mind divide had a paradoxical effect on me. Far from reinforcing me on the merits, it put me in touch with a deep wound—a grief I'd not previously been aware of.

It seems I'd been waiting a long time for someone to see beyond my strength and acknowledge my heart. Unexpectedly, tearfully, I began sharing my hurt over having been misjudged, on many occasions, by people who had made themselves spiritual at my expense.

As if on cue, Louis, seated just to my right, lunged straight for my wannabe heart. With a dagger my own ego had slipped him during a break, he denounced me to the group, as follows: "Adam's so arrogant, he wrote a letter to Scott Peck. He thinks he's on *Peck's* level!" Turning to me, Louis demanded to know how many books *I* had written.

But the tide had turned, and the group was now poised to make hamburger out of Louis for attacking me in my moment of heart.

Lucky for him, my impulse (uncharacteristically) was to head off the massacre. It was suddenly self-evident that Louis (like Gene's mother) was doing the best he could. So I asked everyone just to lighten up and cut him some slack.

I think by this point, we were all running out of steam, and the session petered out rather anticlimactically. But I left it feeling done with my karma as the personification of unloved mind. And glad to have relinquished the unflattering role in which I'd so long been typecast.

27

Relationship Building

Community-building with strangers, in a setting wholly removed from our normal relational context, can only accomplish so much. Despite the intensity (and sincerity) of our emotional outpourings, no piece of our ongoing life's work is present or at risk. Our families and bosses aren't there to test the reality of the love we claim to be sharing.

Thus, the dance we do at events like these should prepare us for something unattainable at the workshop itself. I'd call the goal sustained relational intimacy. In this sense, the workshop sponsor provides a safe environment ("a safe place to be in terror," as one of our Denver FCE participants put it) in which to practice the art of *relationship*-building. But it's only when we get back to our families and jobs that the safety net is removed and the real fun/terror begins.

One of the things I've been mulling since my return from Denver is the difference in my energy *vis-a-vis* Alfred and Louis. As noted above, my reproach to Alfred was harsh even by my usual, unsugarcoated standard. Over the years, it seems, I've come to pride myself in the acuity with which I hold other people's feet to the processing fire. But when Henry's vote of confidence put me in touch with what was driving the acuity, it yielded to a less forceful, more compassionate self-expression.

As I replay this progression in my mind's eye, I realize that appearances to the contrary notwithstanding, none of my interactive dramas has been any less unilateral a *tour de force*. Behind the merits of my every fervent pronouncement lurks this unanswered koan: Does *Adam* (not his putative cause) finally have something he wishes to share? Is he ready, at long last, to be heard? Or, as his fellow barristers might say, is he once again just "making his record"?

The psychospiritual correlatives for this are:

Telling (Making the Record) → Sharing
Listening → Hearing
Facts/Information → Communication
Preaching/Teaching → Reaching

The left side of the arrow is more sensational than relational. And it's the relational quality of the right side that enlivens the interaction, transforming an intellectual or emotional exchange into a heartfelt communication.

I think about the implications of the above for communication in my everyday contexts. What has kept me from seeing that my wife, my children, my partners and employees all are doing the best they can with what they've got . . . and with what I'm currently bringing to the energetic table? So that even as I call them to fulfill (or renegotiate) my righteous expectations, I may yet, please God, at long last, stop *judging* them.

If I could relate to others more right-sidedly, would their "listening" convert to "hearing" in response to my increased "sharing"? Wasn't that the Newtonian essence of the eternal soulmate theory—that a genuine shift in my energy would have to evoke the corresponding response in theirs?

And what if the theory was just wrong? Suppose I made such a quantum individual leap only to disprove, once and for all, the relational hypothesis?

"Well, what have you got to lose?" the nymph of my individual process reprises. "If you can pull it off (and live to share about it), will the relational impact any longer matter?"

About the Author

The author is a former law professor and leading member of the bar. He has also served as cantor of a large, metropolitan synagogue.

"Harofey lishvurey lev umechabeysh l'atzvotam—May our broken hearts be mended, and all our wounds bound up."